Cambridge El

Elements in the Philosophy of Ludwig
edited by
David G. Stern
University of Iowa

WITTGENSTEIN ON KNOWLEDGE AND CERTAINTY

Danièle Moyal-Sharrock
University of Hertfordshire
Duncan Pritchard
University of California, Irvine

CAMBRIDGE UNIVERSITY PRESS

CAMBRIDGE UNIVERSITY PRESS

Shaftesbury Road, Cambridge CB2 8EA, United Kingdom

One Liberty Plaza, 20th Floor, New York, NY 10006, USA

477 Williamstown Road, Port Melbourne, VIC 3207, Australia

314–321, 3rd Floor, Plot 3, Splendor Forum, Jasola District Centre, New Delhi – 110025, India

103 Penang Road, #05–06/07, Visioncrest Commercial, Singapore 238467

Cambridge University Press is part of Cambridge University Press & Assessment, a department of the University of Cambridge.

We share the University's mission to contribute to society through the pursuit of education, learning and research at the highest international levels of excellence.

www.cambridge.org
Information on this title: www.cambridge.org/9781009548090

DOI: 10.1017/9781108946599

© Danièle Moyal-Sharrock and Duncan Pritchard 2024

This publication is in copyright. Subject to statutory exception and to the provisions of relevant collective licensing agreements, no reproduction of any part may take place without the written permission of Cambridge University Press & Assessment.

When citing this work, please include a reference to the DOI 10.1017/9781108946599

First published 2024

A catalogue record for this publication is available from the British Library

ISBN 978-1-009-54809-0 Hardback
ISBN 978-1-108-93119-9 Paperback
ISSN 2632-7112 (online)
ISSN 2632-7104 (print)

Cambridge University Press & Assessment has no responsibility for the persistence or accuracy of URLs for external or third-party internet websites referred to in this publication and does not guarantee that any content on such websites is, or will remain, accurate or appropriate.

Wittgenstein on Knowledge and Certainty

Elements in the Philosophy of Ludwig Wittgenstein

DOI: 10.1017/9781108946599
First published online: December 2024

Danièle Moyal-Sharrock
University of Hertfordshire

Duncan Pritchard
University of California, Irvine

Author for correspondence: Duncan Pritchard, dhpritch@uci.edu

Abstract: An overview is offered of Wittgenstein's groundbreaking discussion of knowledge and certainty, especially in his final notebooks, published as *On Certainty*. The main interpretative readings of *On Certainty* are discussed, especially a non-propositional/non-epistemic interpretation and a variety of propositional and/or epistemic interpretations. Surveys are offered of the readings of *On Certainty* presented by such figures as Annalisa Coliva, John Greco, Danièle Moyal-Sharrock, Duncan Pritchard, Genia Schönbaumsfeld, P. F. Strawson, Michael Williams, and Crispin Wright. This Element demonstrates how *On Certainty* has been especially groundbreaking for epistemology with regard to its treatment of the problem of radical scepticism.

Keywords: Ludwig Wittgenstein, knowledge, certainty, epistemology, scepticism

© Danièle Moyal-Sharrock and Duncan Pritchard 2024

ISBNs: 9781009548090 (HB), 9781108931199 (PB), 9781108946599 (OC)
ISSNs: 2632-7112 (online), 2632-7104 (print)

Contents

Introduction 1

1 Wittgenstein on Knowledge and Certainty 2

2 Hinge Commitments in Contemporary Epistemology 33

List of Abbreviations of Wittgenstein's Works 65

References 67

Introduction

We dedicate this Element to Avrum Stroll.

This Element seeks to elucidate Wittgenstein's groundbreaking discussion of knowledge and certainty and its impact on epistemology, particularly as regards the nature of our most basic commitments and their relevance for the problem of radical scepticism. Our focus will be on Wittgenstein's remarks in his final notebooks, published as *On Certainty*, but the themes being explored reach right back to the *Tractatus* as well as to other works leading to, and broadly contemporaneous with, *On Certainty*.

On Certainty has prompted differing interpretative readings. These differences mostly pertain to the nature of Wittgenstein's notion of certainty. Is it epistemic (a kind of knowledge)? Is it propositional? Is it animal? Is it foundational? Does it succeed in confounding radical scepticism? Philosophers interpret Wittgenstein differently on these issues. And where they agree that Wittgenstein holds a particular view, they sometimes disagree with it.

We think the disparity of views regarding Wittgenstein's reconceptualisation of basic certainty and its relation to knowledge makes co-authorship of this Element a good idea. Its authors – though very close in their understanding of *On Certainty* – differ on some key questions, such as whether our basic certainties are to be understood propositionally. On other issues – such as whether Wittgenstein thought our basic commitments are objects of knowledge and whether he succeeds in confounding radical scepticism – they are fellow travellers.

Wittgenstein's notion of certainty has been gaining wider recognition in philosophy, and we should welcome the recent arrival on the epistemology scene of 'hinge epistemology'.[1] This new branch of epistemology has arisen from the growing acknowledgement that Wittgenstein's notion of basic certainty – these days called 'hinge certainty' for reasons discussed in the Element – raises important questions for, indeed arguably supersedes, mainstream accounts of basic beliefs and radical scepticism. It should also be noted, though the topic of this Element prevents us from engaging the discussion further, that hinge certainty has impacted many disciplines beyond philosophy, such as cognitive science, psychology, gender studies, education, primatology, law, literature and religion.

While both authors have collaborated throughout on producing this manuscript, the Element is divided into two main sections that are primarily authored separately. Section 1 is written by Moyal-Sharrock. It covers the main themes of *On Certainty*, sometimes comparing or contrasting them to pre-*On Certainty* texts. It also makes the case for a non-propositional reading of our basic hinge certainty. Section 2 is written by Pritchard. Its focus is on the way the core ideas

---

[1] See Coliva & Moyal-Sharrock (2017) and Sandis & Moyal-Sharrock (2022).

from *On Certainty* have impacted contemporary epistemology, especially with regard to the recent debate about radical scepticism.

1 Wittgenstein on Knowledge and Certainty

We begin our exploration of Wittgenstein on knowledge and certainty with the words of two philosophers who, each in his own way, importantly contributed to what we know as *On Certainty*: Norman Malcolm and G. H. von Wright. Here is Malcolm, whose discussions with Wittgenstein on Moore's 'A Defence of Common Sense' (1925) and 'Proof of an External World' (1939) were to significantly inspire the notes that make up *On Certainty*:[2]

> *On Certainty* is a brilliant illustration of the novelty of Wittgenstein's thinking. The concepts of certainty and knowledge have received a vast amount of study in the history of philosophy. Wittgenstein presents an entirely fresh way of viewing these concepts. (2018, 671)

As for Von Wright, he was the co-editor – with Elizabeth Anscombe – of the selection of notes that make up *On Certainty*:

> Wittgenstein's treatise on certainty can be said to summarize some of the essential novelties of his thinking. ... The book opens new vistas on his philosophical achievement. (1982, 166)

1.1 The *Tractatus* as Precursor to *On Certainty*

The following paragraph is from von Wright's book *Wittgenstein*:

> In the preface to the *Tractatus*, [*Wittgenstein*] said: ' The book will, therefore, draw a limit to thinking, or rather – not to thinking but to the expression of thoughts; for in order to draw a limit to thinking we should have to be able to think what cannot be thought).' Very much the same thing he could have said in a preface, had he ever written one, to his last writings, those published under the title *On Certainty*. Beyond everything we know or conjecture or think of as true there is a foundation of accepted truth without which there would be no such thing as knowing or conjecturing or thinking things true. But to think of the things, whereof this foundation is made, as **known** to us or as **true** is to place them among the things which stand on this very foundation, is to view the receptacle as another object *within*. This clearly cannot be done. If the foundation is what we have to accept before we say of anything that it is known or true, then it cannot itself be known or true. ... What Moore called 'common sense' ... is very much the same thing as that which Wittgenstein in the *Tractatus* would have referred to as 'the limits of the world'. Wittgenstein's high appreciation of Moore's article must partly have stemmed from the fact

---

[2] See Malcolm (2018), 660–64.

that he recognized in Moore's efforts a strong similarity with his own. And his criticism of Moore in *On Certainty* we could, in the language of the *Tractatus*, characterize as a criticism of an attempt to say the unsayable. (von Wright 1982, 175–76)

Although Wittgenstein came to recant the *Tractatus*,[3] he had sown a seed there which was to grow throughout his philosophy and bloom to full fruition in *On Certainty*. This seed is the realisation that sense has *nonsensical* limits, or foundations: foundations that are not themselves endowed with sense and are not therefore, strictly speaking, *sayable*. That is, they can be verbalized, as one would verbalize a rule, but because a rule is neither true nor false, it is not propositional, not endowed with sense. Later, Wittgenstein will call these limits 'grammar' and expand his notion of grammar to include a brand of certainty that is at the foundation not only of sense, but of knowledge. He will metaphorically compare this certainty to the 'hinges' that must be there for the door of knowledge to turn (OC §343).

Nonsense, the ineffable (or *unsayable*), *grammar, knowledge, certainty*: these are the key notions that will occupy us here. Wittgenstein either modifies or relocates them all. We shall see that certainty becomes, in Wittgenstein's hands, a new animal: often called 'hinge certainty'[4] and, less often, 'objective certainty',[5] it is internally linked to nonsense, ineffability and grammar – all terms that Wittgenstein modifies or refines. As for *knowledge*, Wittgenstein relocates it. In fact, he effects a major shift in epistemology when he divests knowledge (more or less: justified true belief) of its foundational status, which he attributes to *certainty*.

Whereas the early Wittgenstein is concerned with understanding the limits of *sense* – what enables us to make or express sense and can therefore not itself be endowed with sense, the third Wittgenstein[6] will be concerned with the limits or foundations of *knowledge*: what makes knowing possible and cannot therefore itself be an object of knowledge. These foundations, he will call 'grammar' or 'norms of description' (OC §167; §321). Note, however, that for Wittgenstein, grammar is not comprised merely of syntactic rules but of all the conditions for intelligibility: it is the basis from which we can make sense and acquire knowledge. Some of these conditions of intelligibility are due to convention[7]

---

[3] See, for example, Hacker (2001) and Moyal-Sharrock (2007a).
[4] See Coliva & Moyal-Sharrock (2017).
[5] See, for example, Svensson (1981, 84ff) and Stroll (2002, 449ff) who refer exclusively to 'objective certainty'; I initially referred to both 'objective certainty' and 'hinge certainty' (e.g., Moyal-Sharrock 2005), but then used the latter exclusively.
[6] 'The third Wittgenstein' (see Moyal-Sharrock 2004) refers to the post-*Investigations* Wittgenstein: essentially *Remarks* and *Writings on the Philosophy of Psychology, Remarks on Colour* and *On Certainty*.
[7] 'Grammar consists of conventions' (PG §138).

(e.g., 'This is (what we call) a chair'; 'A rod has a length'; '2+2=4'), keeping in mind that conventions are not always due to a concerted consensus, but to an unconcerted agreement in practice. Other conditions for intelligibility are natural or acquired (causally, through enculturation or repeated exposure (OC §143)). These conditions of sense can be verbalised (e.g., 'There exist people other than myself'; 'Human babies cannot feed themselves'). Our meaningful use of words (e.g., 'There are two people in the other room' or 'I'll go feed the baby') is logically based on such norms of description or rules of grammar. They constitute 'the substratum of all [our] enquiring and asserting' (OC §162). 'If the true is what is grounded, then the ground is not *true* nor yet false' (OC §205), writes Wittgenstein. The ground, he will argue in *On Certainty*, is logical or grammatical. We shall have more to say on the logico-grammatical nature of our foundations.

As von Wright put it: 'If the foundation is what we have to accept before we say of anything that it is known or true, then it cannot itself be known or true.' von Wright's use of the word 'accept' is not fortuitous: he wants to avoid describing the foundation as something that results from reasoning or justification, thereby underlining the fact that, for Wittgenstein, knowledge does not go all the way down. What underpins knowledge is what has come to be called, due to this famous metaphor, 'hinge certainty':

> That is to say, the *questions* that we raise and our *doubts* depend on the fact that some propositions are exempt from doubt, are as it were like hinges on which those turn. (OC §341)

Now let us see how some of the seeds of hinge certainty – nonsense, ineffability and grammar – are, as von Wright was right to suggest, sown in Wittgenstein's early work.

1.2 Nonsense, Ineffability and Grammar

What Wittgenstein means by 'nonsense' was the main object of what we might call 'the *Tractatus* wars',[8] which originated with the publication of *The New Wittgenstein* (Crary & Read 2000). In that volume, so-called New Wittgensteinians rebuked 'ineffabilists' – philosophers who, like Peter Hacker, view some nonsense in the *Tractatus* as 'illuminating' – for 'chickening out', for not being 'resolute' enough to recognise that Wittgenstein viewed *all* nonsense as 'plain nonsense'; that is, gibberish. This was unwarranted: Wittgenstein was clear on what he took to be nonsense – and it was not all 'plain nonsense'.

In the *Tractatus*, Wittgenstein viewed as either senseless or nonsensical any expression that does not 'add to our knowledge' (cf. LE 44) – in other words,

---

[8] An expression used by Read & Lavery (2011).

that is not a proposition of natural science (§6.53). The nonsensical included ethics and aesthetics (§6.421), the mystical (§6.522) and his own Tractarian sentences (§6.54). None of these have sense – none are bipolar propositions susceptible of truth and falsity – and cannot therefore add to our knowledge. Indeed, even his own Tractarian sentences do not add to our knowledge; they elucidate (§6.54), which is the rightful task of philosophy (§4.112). Not adding to knowledge makes Tractarian *Sätze* technically nonsensical, devoid of sense. This, however, is a *nonderogatory* use of nonsense. When something does not make sense either because it is *impossible to put into words* (e.g., the mystical, ethics and aesthetics[9]); or because it *enables* or *regulates* sense (e.g., 'There is only one 1' (§4.1272)); or because it *elucidates* (the bounds of) sense (e.g., the nonsensicality of Tractarian remarks), it is nonsensical, in a *nonderogatory* use of the term. In fact, nonsense that regulates sense is one of the early manifestations of what Wittgenstein will later call 'grammar'; and as we shall see, hinge certainties are a later manifestation of regulatory or enabling nonsense. By contrast, nonsense, understood in a derogatory way, results from a *violation* of sense, as when categorial boundaries are misread and allowed to overlap (e.g., 'Is the good more or less identical than the beautiful?' (§4.003); '2+2 at 3 o'clock equals 4' (§4.1272)). *This* nonsense is plain nonsense, gibberish.[10]

It is clear, then, that the *Tractatus* contains different understandings of nonsense, not a uniquely derogatory one.[11] It was a mistake on the part of New Wittgensteinians to insist on a monochrome, 'austere', reading of nonsense as exclusively gibberish. This resulted in viewing Tractarian sentences as gibberish – a consequence they embraced, with no enduring success.

What of ineffability? Inasmuch as in the *Tractatus* Wittgenstein takes only truth-conditional utterances to be sayable (§6.53),[12] any string of words that does not express a truth-conditional proposition is not, technically speaking, *sayable*. On that count, all nonsense is *ineffable*. However, as regards important

---

[9] Ethics, aesthetics and the mystical 'cannot be put into words'. (TLP §6.421; §6.522).

[10] See Moyal-Sharrock (2007a) for a more elaborate discussion of the different uses of nonsense in the *Tractatus*.

[11] The first sentence in the 'Lecture on Ethics' passage (earlier) already shows Wittgenstein alluding to different uses of nonsense; but he was to make this clearer: '[...] the word 'nonsense' is used to exclude certain things [...] for different reasons' (AWL 64). By the time of the *Investigations*, Wittgenstein uses the terms 'nonsense', 'senseless', 'has no sense' indiscriminately to refer to combinations of words that are excluded from the language, 'withdrawn from circulation' (PI §500), and insists that this exclusion may be for different reasons:

> To say 'This combination of words makes no sense (*hat keinen Sinn*)' excludes it from the sphere of language and thereby bounds the domain of language. But when one draws a boundary it may be for various kinds of reason. (PI §499)

[12] '[...] what can be said; i.e. propositions of natural science – i.e. something that has nothing to do with philosophy' (TLP §6.53).

nonsense, the mystical, ethics and aesthetics cannot even be put into words, whereas regulative and elucidatory nonsense, though not *sayable* strictly speaking, can be formulated for heuristic purposes. That is, they can be formulated to serve as steps towards a clearer access to, and demarcation of, the conditions of sense or 'limit to thought' (TLP Preface). This applies to Tractarian remarks, which must be passed over in silence in that they are not hypothetical propositions but the 'steps' or 'ladder' to intelligibility or perspicuity (§6.54). Once used, the ladder must be thrown away (§6.54), for these heuristic aids do not belong to the sphere of language but to its delimitation. They belong to what Wittgenstein will later call the *scaffolding of thought* (OC §211).

The later Wittgenstein will extend the list of the *sayable* to include non-truth-conditional uses of language (e.g., spontaneous utterances, questions, imperatives),[13] but he will never give up the idea that some things cannot meaningfully be *said* 'in the flow of the language-game'; or the idea that some things cannot be put into words *at all* but can only show themselves *through* words (e.g., literary content) and, he will add, through deeds. We shall see that he adds hinge certainties to the list of the ineffable – the grammatical ineffable. All hinge certainties – including such certainties as 'The earth existed long before my birth' (OC §288) – though they appear to be empirical propositions are bounds of sense, not objects of sense; and hence uttering them in the flow of the language game as if they were susceptible of doubt or verification is uttering nonsense, in its *nonderogatory* sense. The same goes for propositions like 'There are physical objects': '"There are physical objects" is nonsense' (OC 35). It is not, however – as Pritchard contends (see, for example, 2.2, 2.4) – *plain* nonsense. I discuss this further in 1.7.

This, then, is how the *Tractatus* sets the stage for what Wittgenstein will later call 'grammar'. The Tractarian 'limits of sense' foreshadow Wittgensteinian grammar, but so do the Tractarian 'limits of the world' foreshadow what Moore called 'common sense' and Wittgenstein will metaphorically call 'background', 'foundations' or 'hinges' – all of which belong to grammar. As Wittgenstein will say: 'everything descriptive of a language-game is part of logic' (OC §56).

1.3 Knowledge Is *Not* Foundational

Wittgenstein's interest in Moore's 'A Defence of Common Sense' (1925) prompted the notes that make up *On Certainty*, and this interest was reawakened by discussions he had with Norman Malcolm in the summer of 1949 in Cornell[14] on that paper and on Moore's 'Proof of an External World' (1939). In these notes, Wittgenstein examines Moore's affirmation that he *knows* such

---

[13] See also (PI §23). [14] See Malcolm (2018).

things as 'Human beings are born and die', 'The earth has existed long before I was born', 'I am standing here', 'I have two hands', 'Here ∅ is a hand'. Moore does not see his inability to *prove* he knows such things as invalidating; he insists that he cannot but 'know' that 'Here ∅ is a hand':

> How absurd it would be to suggest that I did not know it, but only believed it, and that perhaps it was not the case! You might as well suggest that I do not know that I am now standing up and talking . . . . (Moore 1939, 146–47)

On Moore's view, then, we can *know* things that we cannot prove. Indeed, he will claim that all mediated knowledge must eventually terminate in unmediated, or 'immediate knowledge':

> if any proposition whatever is ever known by us mediately, or because some other proposition is known from which it follows, some one proposition at least, must also be known by us immediately, or not merely because some other proposition is known from which it follows. (Moore 1957: 141–42; see also 122–23)

What he calls 'immediate knowledge' is knowledge that is not derived:[15] for the regress to stop, some claims to know must be immediate, not susceptible of justification. For Moore, then, some knowledge is foundational.

Solving the problem of infinite regress is, of course, crucial, but one ought not do so by insisting that therefore *knowledge* must be basic. Moore's notion of 'immediate knowledge' has been questioned,[16] but the real problem lies in seeking to revamp 'knowledge' in the first place. For the concept of knowledge as involving some variant of truth and justification has had a prosperous history and continues to serve (as even Gettier recognized). Rather than attempting to repair the perennial regress problem by reconceptualising knowledge, divesting it of its longstanding components, we should instead ask what more fundamental doxastic attitude might be underpinning it. This is what Wittgenstein does in *On Certainty*. He takes on Moore's supercilious challenge – 'You might as well suggest that I do not know that I am now standing up and talking' (1939, 147):

> I should like to say: Moore does not *know* what he asserts he knows, but it stands fast for him, as also for me; regarding it as absolutely solid is part of our *method* of doubt and enquiry. (OC §151)

> . . . how do I *know* that it is my hand? Do I even here know exactly what it means to say it is my hand? – When I say 'how do I know?' I do not mean that

---

[15] Another notable attempt at a sort of immediate knowledge was Bertrand Russell's 'knowledge by acquaintance' which he distinguished from 'knowledge by description' (Russell 1910; 1912: Ch. 5).
[16] See, for example, Malmgrem (1983).

> I have the least *doubt* of it. What we have here is a foundation for all my action. But it seems to me that it is wrongly expressed by the words 'I know'. (OC §414)

> To say of man, in Moore's sense, that he *knows* something; that what he says is therefore unconditionally the truth, seems wrong to me. – It is the truth only inasmuch as it is an unmoving foundation of his language-games. (OC §403)

Wittgenstein is clear: Moore does not *know* that he is now standing up and talking or that what he is waving is a hand. He refers to his assurance of these things as 'knowledge' because that is to him the concept that expresses the greatest degree of conviction on our epistemic spectrum. Wittgenstein agrees that Moore's assurance is indubitable; but disagrees that it is knowledge. This is because knowing is for Wittgenstein – as it is in our epistemic practices – an achievement; something we come to; something of which we can retrace the steps and invoke the grounds:

> One says 'I know' when one is ready to give compelling grounds. 'I know' relates to a possibility of demonstrating the truth. (OC §243)

> [When] Moore says he knows the earth existed etc., ... has he ... got the right *ground* for his conviction? For if not, then after all he doesn't *know*. (OC §91)

Only in very special circumstances, such as after an accident, is it possible for someone to *find out* or *make sure* that they have two hands:

> If I don't know whether someone has two hands (say, whether they have been amputated or not) I shall believe his assurance that he has two hands, if he is trustworthy. And if he says he *knows* it, that can only signify to me that he has been able to make sure, and hence that his arms are e.g. not still concealed by coverings and bandages, etc. etc. My believing the trustworthy man stems from my admitting that it is possible for him to make sure. (OC §23)

Outside of such special circumstances, it is not possible to make sure that one has two hands; and, therefore, not possible to *know* it. However, as Malcolm recounts, Wittgenstein makes a concession: there *can* be uses of 'I know' where it is *not* sensible to speak of 'making sure', but only outside of philosophical contexts:

> There is an ordinary use of 'I know' when there isn't any making sure. For example, a sighted person could say it to a blind man who asks 'Are you sure that it's a tree?' And also when we have completed an investigation we can say, 'I know now that it's a tree.' Another example: if you and I were coming through woods towards a house and I broke out into the clearing and there was the house right before me, I might exclaim 'There's the house.' You, back in the bushes, might ask doubtfully 'Are you sure?', and I should reply 'I

know it.' Here the use of 'I know it' would be natural, and yet it would also be a case of certainty 'in the highest degree', a case in which I should be willing to count nothing as evidence that there isn't a house there. Moore might have given such examples, examples of a use of 'I know' in which that expression really functions '*im sprachlichen Verkehr*', i.e., in the actual traffic of language, in 'the stream of life.' But he doesn't give such examples: he prefers to gaze at a tree and say 'I know there's a tree there.' And this is because he wants to give himself the experience of knowing. (Malcolm 2018, 662)

Wittgenstein, then, does admit the use of 'I know' in ordinary life to convey indubitable certainty, or 'certainty "in the highest degree"' as he puts it, but he will not countenance it in *philosophical* contexts:

> What I am aiming at is also found in the difference between the casual observation 'I know that that's a ... ', as it might be used in ordinary life, and the same utterance when a philosopher makes it. (OC §406)

> For when Moore says 'I know that that's ... ' I want to reply 'you don't *know* anything!' – and yet I would not say that to anyone who was speaking without philosophical intention. That is, I feel (rightly?) that these two mean to say something different. (OC §407)

For Wittgenstein, we should not interfere with the ordinary use of language, and therefore not correct the casual use of 'I know' in *ordinary* cases of indubitable certainty; but a philosopher should, in philosophical argument, be more conceptually responsible. A philosopher's claim to 'know' in indubitable cases – by invoking immediate knowledge, acquaintance or awareness – is misguided. As Wittgenstein sees it, Moore – like Russell before him[17] – has a confused picture of knowledge. He takes knowledge to be something one experiences; he falls prey to 'the tendency to think of knowledge as a *mental state*'.[18] According to Wittgenstein, reports Malcolm:

> Moore would like to stare at a house that is only 20 feet away and say, with a peculiar intonation, 'I know that there's a house!' He does this because he wants to produce in himself the feeling of knowing. ... It is as if someone had said 'You don't really feel pain when you are pinched' and Moore then pinched himself in order to feel the pain, and thus prove to himself that the other is wrong. Moore treats the sentence 'I know so & so' like the sentence 'I have a pain'. (Malcolm 2018, 660)

Whereas the ordinary use of 'I know' *usually* arises from making sure, the philosophical use of 'I know' must *always* result from some investigative or

---

[17] For Wittgenstein's criticism of Russell's notion of 'intuitive awareness', see CE, including Appendix A.
[18] In Malcolm (2018, 660).

ratiocinative process. The philosopher must be aware that, in default circumstances,[19] one's being in the country one lives in, or one's certainty of having a body, or there existing people other than oneself, cannot be a result of investigation and cannot therefore be an object of knowledge.

And so, Moore was right about the indubitability of some of our beliefs not being due to justification, but he was wrong to call it 'knowledge'. The background, or substratum, of our thoughts (OC §62; §194) is not something we hold as *true* or come to *know*; it is a given: an 'inherited' or *assumed* background:

> I did not get my picture of the world by satisfying myself of its correctness nor do I have it because I am satisfied of its correctness. No: it is the inherited background against which I distinguish between true and false. (OC §94)

> If I say '*we assume* that the earth has existed for many years past' (or something similar), then of course it sounds strange that we should *assume* such a thing. But in the entire system of our language-games it belongs to the foundations. The assumption,[20] one might say, forms the basis of action, and therefore, naturally, of thought. (OC §411)

> For why should the language-game rest on some kind of knowledge? (OC §477)

It should be clear, then, that Wittgenstein's conception of knowledge is the traditional one: knowledge as justified true belief.[21] As I have suggested, and will show, what lies at the foundation of thought and action is certainty, not knowledge. However, some Wittgensteinians do not take certainty to be foundational, claiming instead – explicitly or implicitly – that, for Wittgenstein too, some knowledge is foundational. For Michael Williams: 'basic certainties are basic knowledge, on an "infallibilist" conception of knowledge' (2021a, 179); 'Wittgenstein's epistemology is "knowledge first"' (2021b, 140); 'groundless knowledge' (2021a, 194). Genia Schönbaumsfeld (2016, 116), rather than distinguish between 'certainty' and 'knowledge', proposes to 'distinguish between a "logical" and an "epistemic" sense of 'to know'. Annalisa Coliva (2013, 2–3) finds three possible uses of 'I know' and 'knowledge' in *On Certainty*: an empirical, a grammatical and a nonsensical use; and suggests that Wittgenstein has the grammatical use in mind when saying that certainties can be known.

---

[19] That is, outside exceptional circumstances such as pathological or fictional ones.
[20] Wittgenstein further clarifies his use of 'assumption':

> But it isn't that the situation is like this: We just *can't* investigate everything, and for that reason we are forced to rest content with assumption. If I want the door to turn, the hinges must stay put. (OC §343)

Hinge certainties are assumptions in that they 'go without saying' (OC §568), not in that they are believed to be true or probably true without proof.

[21] Though see Glock (2016) and Schroeder (2024).

Wittgenstein, as we know, encouraged us to 'show differences'. Instead, we are here recommended to use a single concept in diverse, mutually exclusive, ways. This may do – albeit at the risk of ambiguity and confusion – for ordinary language, but it cannot do for philosophical elucidation. It is precisely this kind of *pot pourri* of 'knowledge' that Wittgenstein is attempting to wean us, and himself, from in *On Certainty* when he says he wants to reply to Moore: '"you don't *know* anything!" – and yet I would not say that to anyone who was speaking without philosophical intention' (OC §407). It seems very difficult, however, for epistemologists to give up on the supremacy and primacy of knowledge: 'One is often bewitched by a word. For example, by the word "know"' (OC §435).

Before going further, we should note that, inasmuch as 'epistemic' means 'related to knowledge' and 'epistemological' means 'related to the branch in philosophy we call "epistemology"', to speak of 'hinge epistemology' is to say that 'hinges' (or hinge certainties) have a role to play in epistemology; it does not, however, imply that hinges are epistemic.

1.4 Hinge Certainty: Logical, Not Epistemic

Wittgenstein's notes were entitled *Über Gewissheit* (*On Certainty*) because his attempts to find a better description for our most fundamental assurance – what Moore takes to be 'knowledge' – repeatedly involve talk of 'certainty' and cognate terms. In German, Wittgenstein uses not only *Gewissheit,* but also *Sicherheit,* and other related expressions: *Bestimmtheit* ('certainty'); *Versicherung* ('assurance'); *Überzeugung* ('conviction'); *(das) Sichersein* ('being sure'); *unbedingt vertrauen* ('trust without reservation'); *Glaube* ('belief'); '*es steht (für mich) fest*': 'it stands fast (for me).' In the process, he also distinguishes *objective* from *subjective* certainty:

> With the word 'certain' we express complete conviction, the total absence of doubt, and thereby we seek to convince other people. That is *subjective* certainty.
> But when is something objectively certain? When a mistake is not possible. But what kind of possibility is that? Mustn't mistake be *logically* excluded? (OC §194)

Subjective certainty is not what Wittgenstein is after. For, although the certainty he is striving to define is a certainty that stands fast for us individually ('I act with *complete* certainty. But this certainty is my own' (OC §174)), it cannot be merely personal ('But it isn't just that *I* believe in this way that I have two hands, but that every reasonable person does' (OC §252)). Complete conviction, the total absence of doubt, suffices for someone to be subjectively certain (OC §194), but if the claim to certainty is to be more than a subjective claim, the certainty needs to be objectively established:

> It needs to be *shewn* that no mistake was possible. Giving the assurance 'I know' doesn't suffice. For it is after all only an assurance that I can't be making a mistake, and it needs to be *objectively* established that I am not making a mistake about *that*. (OC §15)

But if *objectively* establishing that we are not making a mistake about something is merely giving grounds for our conviction ('"I have compelling grounds for my certitude." These grounds make the certitude objective' (OC §270)), then the claim to objective certainty is not really distinguishable from the claim to knowledge. Moreover, an objective certainty that is *based on grounds* – compelling or not – is susceptible of mistake: 'For there can be dispute whether something *is* certain; I mean, when something is *objectively* certain' (OC §273). The only objective certainty that would be categorially distinct from knowing is one whose imperviousness to mistake and doubt would not be grounded at all, but *logical*:

> The difference between the concept of 'knowing' and the concept of 'being certain' isn't of any great importance at all, except where 'I know' is meant to mean: I *can't* be wrong. (OC §8)

> But when is something objectively certain? When a mistake is not possible. But what kind of possibility is that? Mustn't mistake be *logically* excluded? (OC §194)

Only an 'objective certainty' that is groundless and logically indubitable – that is, a *nonepistemic* certainty – would allow Wittgenstein to say that: '"[k]nowledge" and "certainty" belong to different *categories*' (OC §308). And so, in order not to court ambiguity, I refer to that specific brand of 'objective certainty' as 'hinge certainty'.

Note that the notion of certainty that emerges in *On Certainty* had made budding appearances in earlier texts. Particularly – but not only[22] – in 'Cause and Effect', the Big Typescript and *Philosophical Investigations*:

> The primitive form of the language game is certainty, not uncertainty. For uncertainty could never lead to action. (CE 397)

> The fire will burn me if I stick my hand in it: that is certainty.

---

[22] For more passages mentioning certainty and related notions in earlier Wittgenstein manuscripts, see van Gennip(2008). As I argue in my Introduction to Moyal-Sharrock (2004), these passages do not preclude the notion of a 'third Wittgenstein', predicated not only on OC but on all post-PI 'works'.

> That is to say: here you see what certainty means. (Not only what the word 'certainty' means, but also what certainty is all about.)
> The belief that fire will burn me is of the same nature as the fear that it will burn me.
> If I were dragged into a fire I would resist and not go willingly; likewise I would shout: 'It's going to burn me!', not: 'Maybe it will be quite pleasant!' (BT 180)

> 'The certainty that the fire will burn me is based on induction.' Does that mean that I argue to myself: 'Fire has always burned me, so it will happen now too?' Or is the previous experience the *cause* of my certainty, not its ground? (PI §325)

In spite of the numerous references to 'certainty' throughout *On Certainty*, Schönbaumsfeld (2017, 108) does not believe that we are here in the presence of *any kind of certainty*: '"hinges" are best not conceived as certainties ... at all.' Evidently, Wittgenstein did not share this view. Not only does he call it that – (e.g., 'If you tried to doubt everything you would not get as far as doubting anything. The game of doubting itself presupposes certainty' (OC §115)) – his use of 'certainty' is not, as Schönbaumsfeld contends, categorially alien to other uses of 'certainty' or indeed to some uses of 'belief', 'trust' and 'faith'. We speak of 'belief in', 'trust' and 'faith' as doxastic attitudes and hinge certainty resembles these in being, as we shall see, a non-propositional attitude; but he also extends from these uses in that, in the case of hinge certainty, something not 'standing fast' for someone does not result in uncertainty or mistake but reflects their being prey to pathology:

> For months I have lived at address A, I have read the name of the street and the number of the house countless times, have received countless letters here and given countless people the address. If I am wrong about it, the mistake is hardly less than if I were (wrongly) to believe I was writing Chinese and not German. (OC §70)

> If my friend were to imagine one day that he had been living for a long time past in such and such a place, etc. etc., I should not call this a *mistake*, but rather a mental disturbance, perhaps a transient one. (OC §71)

Granted, Wittgenstein struggles to find the right words to describe our basic assurance, but the ones he *does* contemplate and ends up using are epistemological concepts that are also susceptible of *non-epistemic* and *non-propositional* use: concepts like certainty, belief and trust. Those three he does not reject. The concept that is *not* thus susceptible – that is, knowledge – he rejects in the very first passage of *On Certainty*: 'If you do know that *here is one hand*, we'll grant you all the rest'; and goes on rejecting it throughout.

1.5 No Grounds, No Doubt, No Scepticism

We saw that Wittgenstein's view of knowledge is the standard view: knowledge requires grounds – indeed, the right grounds (OC §91). But what is less standard is his view that doubt, too, requires grounds:[23]

> 'I know that I am a human being.' In order to see how unclear the sense of this proposition is, consider its negation. . . . what about such a proposition as 'I know I have a brain'? Can I doubt it? Grounds for *doubt* are lacking! (OC §4)
>
> What we can ask is whether it makes sense to doubt it. (OC §2)

Just as 'the concept of knowing is coupled with that of the language-game' (OC §560), so is the concept of doubt:

> The idealist's question would be something like: 'What right have I not to doubt the existence of my hands?' (And to that the answer can't be: I *know* that they exist.) But someone who asks such a question is overlooking the fact that a doubt about existence only works in a language-game. Hence, that we should first have to ask: what would such a doubt be like?, and don't understand this straight off. (OC §24)

That 'a doubt about existence only works in a language-game' means that doubt cannot be gratuitous or idle; it requires reasons; or, as Olli Lagerspetz (2021, 39) puts it, 'some investigative context'. The absence of coherent grounds makes one's 'doubt' incoherent:

> If someone said that he doubted the existence of his hands, kept looking at them from all sides, tried to make sure it wasn't 'all done by mirrors', etc., we should not be sure whether we ought to call that doubting. We might describe his way of behaving as like the behaviour of doubt, but his game would not be ours. (OC §255)

Not all that has the *appearance* of doubt *is* doubt. In some cases, what looks like doubt is only *doubt behaviour*. Of course, where doubt has no rational motivation or justification, it may have (pathological) *causes* (OC §74), but normal doubt must have *reasons*. It isn't enough to *say* or *imagine* we doubt: genuine doubt, like suspicion, must have *grounds*. (OC §322, §458)

Wittgenstein's recognition that the sceptic's radical doubt is only doubt behaviour is spurred by his realisation that were her doubt not hinged on some certainty, the sceptic could not even formulate it:

---

[23] Here is Tiercelin (2010, 1, my translation):

> We owe to both Peirce and Wittgenstein to have stressed, with uncommon emphasis, that doubt, as much as belief, requires *reasons*. For both, scepticism's mistake consists in not asking why, how, and with what help we are able to doubt (OC §125).

> If I wanted to doubt whether or not this was my hand, how could I avoid doubting whether the word 'hand' has any meaning? So that is something I seem to *know* after all. (OC §369)

> But more correctly: The fact that I use the word 'hand' and all the other words in my sentence without a second thought, indeed that I should stand before the abyss if I wanted so much as to try doubting their meanings – shews that absence of doubt belongs to the essence of the language-game, that the question 'How do I know …' drags out the language-game, or else does away with it. (OC §370)

Interestingly, the germ of Wittgenstein's recognition that the sceptic's affirmation is nonsense – it is an affirmation that cancels itself out – can be found in the *Tractatus*:

> Scepticism is *not* irrefutable, but obviously nonsensical, when it tries to raise doubts where no questions can be asked.
> For doubt can exist only where a question exists, a question only where an answer exists, and an answer only where something *can be said*. (TLP §6.51)

How can radical doubt make sense when the very possibility of formulating a question rests on the indubitability of the meaning of the words used to formulate it? If something cannot be doubted, radical doubt is out of the question.

Its being essential to our making sense means that certainty underpins all our questions and doubts (OC 341), including the sceptic's alleged radical doubt, thereby invalidating it:

> A doubt that doubted everything would not be a doubt. (OC §450)

> If you tried to doubt everything you would not get as far as doubting anything. The game of doubting itself presupposes certainty. (OC §115)

Certainty is not optional or merely desirable: it is conceptually necessary for doubt to even be formulated. This makes radical scepticism conceptually impossible: 'our *doubts* depend on the fact that some propositions are exempt from doubt, are as it were like hinges on which those turn' (OC §341). Radical doubt must be called out for what it is: the mere mouthing of doubt; *doubt-behaviour*.

Radical scepticism is not sustainable; and this, not for pragmatic, but for conceptual or logical reasons. Also, we might add, for existential reasons. If we consider Pyrrhonism, which is allegedly a lived scepticism – that is, scepticism as stance rather than as intellectual claim – we might ask: can it really be *lived*? It might be argued, as does R. J. Hankinson, that suspension of judgement is compatible with living:

> Faced with endemic dispute, Sceptics reserve judgment; but this does not render life impossible for them, since they will still react to the way things appear to be, although without believing in any strong sense that things really are as they seem. (Hankinson 1998)

Well, they may not believe *in a strong sense*, but they *act* in a strong sense. They have to, in order to survive. Prefixing a judgement with 'it seems to' does not mean I really suspend judgement if I act on that judgement anyway: 'it seems to be raining outside', and I take an umbrella; 'it seems to me I'm hungry', and I eat. This sounds very much like a case of the 'mouthing' of suspension of belief. As Duncan Pritchard explains (in conversation): 'Pyrrhonism exempts a wide class of propositions from doubt, which is why it isn't radical – this is what enables it to be a lived stance.' And so, *radical* scepticism is simply untenable, in theory or in life.

The threat of radical scepticism has needlessly exercised epistemologists for centuries. At 'the foundation of all operating with thoughts (with language)' (OC §401) is a certainty endorsed every time a doubt (towards it) is formulated.[24] This is a knock-down objection to radical scepticism. And yet radical scepticism survives. Why? I think, for two reasons. The first is that many epistemologists are loathe to give up on the primacy and supremacy of knowledge and to accept the non-epistemic status of basic beliefs. Let us look at a version of the sceptic's paradoxical argument:

Premise 1: We are unable to know the denials of sceptical hypotheses.
Premise 2: If we are unable to know the denials of sceptical hypotheses, then we are unable to know anything of substance about the world.
Conclusion: We are unable to know anything of substance about the world.

It is the prerogative of an unsound argument to have a valid paradoxical conclusion. What Wittgenstein has done is show the sceptic that her argument is unsound; that its premise – for example, that we are unable to *know* the denials of radical sceptical hypotheses – is confused or nonsensical or idle. Let us, once more, recall von Wright's words: 'If the foundation is what we have to accept before we say of anything that it is known or true, then it cannot itself be known or true.' This is the logical condition that the sceptic is unwilling to recognise when she requires that we *know* the denials of radical sceptical hypotheses. And so, her sceptical argument – inasmuch as it requires us to *know* something in order to be able to know anything else – is confused. Indeed,

---

[24] This may be seen as a variation of Descartes's acknowledgement that the very fact of being able to conceive of, or formulate 'I am' (*cogito*) necessitates its 'truth' (*ergo sum*). Whether what is being formulated is a doubt (as in the sceptical case) or an affirmation makes no difference to the very possibility of coherent formulation implying or necessitating some hinge certainty.

the strength of the hold knowledge has on epistemologists is such that even those who agree with Wittgenstein about the groundlessness of our basic certainties feel a kind of vertigo in experiencing that groundlessness.[25]

Another reason, I suggest, for the persistence of radical scepticism is that conceivability (or imaginability) is deemed, by many philosophers, sufficient for possibility. So that sci-fi scenarios, such as brain-in-a-vat (BIV) scenarios, are viewed as rational possibilities that must be contended with and argued against rather than dismissed as what Williams (2017) rightly calls 'fairy-tale imaginings'.[26] And dismissed they must be, for – as Angélique Thébert (2023) reminds us in 'Peut-on comprendre le sceptique?' ('Can the sceptic be understood?') – they do not include the forms of life necessary to meaning. Sceptical scenarios have no grip because the described situation – so detached is it from the 'stream of life' which soaks utterances with meaning – is what Jean Bazin (2002, 132 & 134) calls an 'experimental vacuum' or a 'non situation'. This is why, though we may express belief in sceptical scenarios (that beckon us to imagine a being outside the context of a world), we do not *really* believe them; for, they do not take place in 'anthropological space' ('l'espace anthropologique')[27] (2023, 327–28). As Thébert writes:

> Sceptical discourse is not empowered by any social practices. Outside its bounds as thought experiment, it ceases to fascinate us and shows itself in its true light; that is, as a slice of inert discourse ('frozen, deactivated'), because 'extracted and disjuncted'[28] from the shared practices necessary for sense. We are, with the sceptic, on the same ground as with Wittgenstein's imagined Martian (OC §430) – that is, on empty ground. . . . In the end, what leads us astray is the fact that it is philosophers who give voice to such a sceptic. We take the sceptic's words to reflect a mastery of language, and beyond that, a mastery of the social practices that are implied by the mastery of language, whereas, in fact, the sceptic is presented to us in the utmost solitude and bareness. . . . In fact, we understand the sceptic only as a character in a fictive construction, a thought experiment created and narrated by a philosopher. However, outside this strictly delimited context which is 'shared ludic pretense', her words are . . . incomprehensible. (2023, 328–31 *passim*; my translation).

Radical sceptical scenarios are therefore what Pritchard (2012, 126) calls 'unmotivated error possibilit[ies]'. They are unmotivated – that is, as Wittgenstein might put it, 'idle' or 'otiose' – in that they are not backed by, and therefore pertinent to, our human form of life and are therefore humanly meaningless.

---

[25] See Pritchard (2015a, part 4, 2019b, 2020) for a discussion of *epistemic vertigo*.
[26] See also Moyal-Sharrock (2003), Schönbaumsfeld (2017) and Thébert (2023).
[27] Bazin (2002, 137).   [28] Bazin (2002, 141).

One of Wittgenstein's 'right point[s] of attack' (OC 36) against the sceptic is her belief that the indubitability of our basic certainties is epistemic; that it is a knowing. Another (related) point which the sceptic needs to accept is that doubt can only work in a language-game, which is to say that doubt or error must be motivated. As we have seen, they are not. And so, the scenarios concocted by the sceptic are logically idle; not serious, pertinent, possible, threats.

Genia Schönbaumsfeld (2016) defends the thesis that radical scepticism is an illusion by aiming to dispel the engrained notion that radical scepticism poses a real problem for epistemology, and therefore that it needs solving. Her position is that radical scepticism is 'an apparent claim (or set of claims) that one cannot "refute" – that is, show to be false – as it never adds up to a genuine, substantial position in the first place', and so there is 'in the end, no "global" sceptical scenario that requires a solution' (Schönbaumsfeld 2016, 1). As Claudine Tiercelin has it:

> ...it is less a question of 'refuting' the sceptic than of diagnosing the roots of her illusion and the roots of our attraction to the illusion. The whole point is to find out what the status of these beliefs, and our relationship to them, is. (Tiercelin 2010, 13; my translation)

Indeed, showing the sceptic the roots of her illusion is tantamount to debunking scepticism.

I would say that the two single most important insights responsible for Wittgenstein's understanding of the nature of our basic beliefs is that not everything that has the *appearance* of doubt *is* doubt; and that not everything that has the *appearance* of an empirical proposition is one: in some cases, *what look like* empirical or experiential propositions are logical bounds of sense, and so *cannot* be doubted or refuted. Having discussed the first insight, let us look more closely at the latter.

1.6 The Non-Empirical and Non-Propositional Nature of Hinges

At some point, 'justification comes to an end' (OC §192). There, where the spade turns, is the rock solid ground of our indubitable certainties. Indubitable not because they have been proved true beyond doubt, but because they are *logically* impervious to doubt:

> 'There are cases where doubt is unreasonable, but others where it seems logically impossible.' (OC §454)

> 'I cannot doubt this proposition without giving up all judgment.'
> But what sort of proposition is that? ... It is certainly no empirical proposition. It does not belong to psychology. It has rather the character of a rule. (OC §494).

By 'rule', Wittgenstein means a norm of description; a grammatical or logical rule. What Wittgenstein is realizing is that Moore-type propositions, though they *look like* empirical propositions, are in fact expressions of our logical bounds of sense:

> When Moore says he *knows* such and such, he is really enumerating a lot of empirical propositions which we affirm without special testing; propositions, that is, which have a peculiar logical role in the system of our empirical propositions. (OC §136)

And so, to express doubt towards them amounts to nonsense: 'If Moore were to pronounce the opposite of those propositions which he declares certain, we should not just not share his opinion: we should regard him as demented' (OC §155).

It takes Wittgenstein some time to reach the conclusion that what look like empirical propositions are not empirical propositions. He begins by contemplating the idea that *some empirical propositions have a logical status*. Here is Malcolm reporting Wittgenstein's words:

> Experiential propositions do not all have the same logical status. With regard to some, of which we say that we *know* them to be true, we can imagine circumstances on the basis of which we should say that the statement had turned out to be false. But with others there are no circumstances in which we should say 'it turned out to be false.' This is a logical remark and has nothing to do with what I shall say ten minutes from now. Moore's propositions – 'I know that I am a human being', 'I know that the earth has existed for many years', etc. – have this characteristic, that it is impossible to think of circumstances in which we should allow that we have evidence against them. . . . The sceptical philosophers . . . interpret Moore's 'I know it with absolute certainty' as an expression of extreme conviction. What is needed is to show them that the highest degree of certainty is nothing psychological but something logical: that there is a point at which there is neither any 'making more certain' nor any 'turning out to be false'. Some experimental statements have this property. . . . Certain propositions belong to my 'frame of reference'. If I had to give *them* up, I shouldn't be able to judge *anything*. Take the example of the earth's having existed for many years before I was born. What evidence against it could there be? A document? (Malcolm 2018, 662–63)

In *On Certainty*, Wittgenstein further contemplates the possibility of a hybrid status: 'Is it that rule and empirical proposition merge into one another?' (OC §309). But his answer is negative: it is not that rule and empirical proposition merge into one another, but that *what looks like* an empirical proposition is not always one:

That is, we are interested in the fact that about certain empirical propositions no doubt can exist if making judgments is to be possible at all. Or again: I am inclined to believe that not everything that has the form of an empirical proposition *is* one. (OC §308)[29]

As Malcolm writes: 'Ludwig Wittgenstein, in discussion, gave me the principal idea of this paper – namely, that there is a resemblance in logic between some *a priori* and some empirical statements' (1952, 189). Wittgenstein's answer to the possibility of a hybrid proposition-rule is that we are here misled by *form*; these seemingly empirical propositions about which no doubt can exist if making judgements is to be possible are not propositions at all but expressions of grammatical rules: they 'form the foundation of all operating with thoughts (with language)' (OC §401).

However, some interpreters take Wittgenstein to mean that hinge certainties are indeed a hybrid of empirical proposition and rule. For Tiercelin (2010, 7), because the indubitable trust we have in 'these indubitable propositions' is not derived from, nor grounded in, experience (OC §§130–31), but is rather due to their role as rules and norms, they are 'pseudo-empirical propositions.' Similarly, Annalisa Coliva (2010, 80) views hinges as 'Janus-faced', as she puts it; they are *judgements* (and therefore truth-conditional propositions) that play a *normative* role (and are therefore non-propositional); they are, like rules, exempt from doubt. Coliva's view is not the one, explicitly voiced by Wittgenstein, that the same sentence can at one time express a judgement and at another a rule of testing (OC §98), but that a hinge is both at once: 'Here is my

---

[29] To the questioned suitability of taking OC §308 to be answering OC §309 (as §308 obviously comes first), two replies can be made: a general and a specific one. The general one is that *On Certainty* should not be read as a single, continuous or linear argument, but as consisting of the repeated reformulations of a small number of questions, prompting the contemplation of various answers and the (repeated) adoption of some. This method of philosophizing is such that Wittgenstein does not allow previous answers to be retained or carried over to the next set of questioning; rather the same problems are surveyed again and again, afresh, naively, from different perspectives. This, incidentally, is not only true of the remarks that make up *On Certainty*, but of most of Wittgenstein's post-Tractarian work. In the Preface to *Philosophical Investigations*, he writes: 'The same or almost the same points were always being approached afresh from different directions, and new sketches made' (Preface, v). And so, the fact that Wittgenstein has answered a question does not stop him from asking it – or rather a reformulation of it – again. A specific reply to the objection is that the answer given by §308, as indeed the question asked at §309, are to be found again later, at OC §319:

But wouldn't one have to say then, that there is no sharp boundary between propositions of logic and empirical propositions? The lack of sharpness *is* that of the boundary between *rule* and empirical proposition. (OC §319)

We now have two clear instances of Wittgenstein's replying negatively to the question of whether our basic certainties are instances of empirical propositions and rules merging into one another. There are more.

hand', 'The earth has existed for a very long time', 'My name is AC' ... play a normative role, *while also being judgements*' (2010a, 142; my emphasis). In 2.5, Pritchard discusses Coliva's view of 'extended rationality'.

But rather than take a hinge certainty to be simultaneously (and therefore paradoxically) a judgement and the rule that enables that judgement, I suggest extending Wittgenstein's notion that a sentence does not wear its *meaning* on its sleeve to the notion that a sentence does not wear its *status* on its sleeve. Just as the meaning of a sentence is dependent on use, so is the *status* of a sentence dependent on use. The very same sentence can have different meanings and/or statuses depending on its use or context. And so, rather than view hinges as 'Janus-faced', we should understand that identical sentences, or *Doppelgänger*, can function in some contexts as a hinge and in other contexts as an empirical or an epistemic proposition. A sentence cannot, however, function as both in precisely the same context (e.g., at the same time for the same person): if someone asked me to hold still in the adjacent room while they were switching on the alarm, and I shouted back: 'I am not moving', that sentence would be a formulation of my hinge certainty that I was not moving, while at the same time function for the other person as an empirical proposition. But the sentence cannot be both the expression of a hinge and of an empirical proposition *at the same time, for me*. As Wittgenstein makes clear: 'If you measure a table with a yardstick, are you also measuring the yardstick? If you are measuring the yardstick, then you cannot be measuring the table at the same time' (RFM III 74, p. 199).

Hinges cannot, *qua* hinges, be both judgement and rule (or norm). Their having the role of rules makes hinges non-propositional. Coliva (2010, 172–73), however, takes hinges to be both non-propositional and propositional: 'Hence, the question is: how do the propositional and the non-propositional account of certainty go together, if they do?' I do not believe they do. Propositions are truth-evaluable and hinges – being rules, or bounds of sense – are not.

Like Coliva, Schönbaumsfeld takes hinges to be both propositional and non-propositional. Despite referring to them as 'hinge propositions', Schönbaumsfeld (2016, 116) agrees that we have here to do with expressions of rules of grammar: 'one might say that "hinge propositions" are an attempt to articulate the logical enabling conditions that allow our epistemic practices to operate, and without which even our words could not mean anything'. They are 'logical enabling conditions rather than ordinary empirical propositions' (Schönbaumsfeld 2016, 128). But what would be an *extra*ordinary empirical proposition?

To defend their positions, Coliva and Schönbaumsfeld appeal to Wittgenstein calling them 'propositions' (*Sätze*) in several passages of *On Certainty*. Indeed, he does – and this is due to the fact that he is in the process of understanding the nature of Moore-type 'propositions', and to the fact that the German word 'Satz' can be translated as both 'sentence' and 'proposition'. It does not, however, prevent Wittgenstein from clearly coming to realize that they are *not* propositions: 'the end is not certain propositions striking us immediately as true i. e. it is not a kind of *seeing* on our part; it is our *acting*, which lies at the bottom of the language-game' (OC §204). The enactive status of hinges is further discussed in 1.7.

Because there are passages in *On Certainty* that back Schönbaumsfeld's and Coliva's decisions to call hinges 'propositions', and other passages that back rejecting it, the matter cannot be settled by a mere show of passages; it must be bolstered by more substantive argument. The argument is as follows: we must go beyond Wittgenstein's deliberative and heuristic uses of some of the terms in *On Certainty* (such as 'proposition', 'know' or 'trust') to see where he *ends up* – that is, what he ultimately thinks about using such terms or concepts to describe the kind of certainty in question here. Some passages formulate his ultimate insights clearly enough; for example, OC §204 (earlier) as regards 'proposition'; or this, as regards 'knowing':

> I should like to say: Moore does not *know* what he asserts he knows, but it stands fast for him, as also for me; regarding it as absolutely solid is part of our *method* of doubt and enquiry. (OC §151)

Wittgenstein's groundbreaking account of hinge certainty – the account which, in recognising the non-epistemic and non-propositional nature of our basic certainties, puts an end to the regress problem of basic beliefs and demonstrates the incoherence of radical scepticism – is dependent on such passages and this makes their importance a matter of fact, not a matter of interpretational preference. Attributing the account to the interpreter would amount to crediting her with the achievement. The endgame as to which features are retained and which are not cannot hang on the interpreter's predilection, but on the coherence and overall merit of the interpretation. Coliva (2016, 81) is right to say that, when all is said and done, Wittgenstein's remarks ought to be 'assessed on philosophical merit.'

Terminological red herrings should not, therefore, detract us from concluding that doing away with the propositional nature of our basic certainties is the key achievement of *On Certainty*. Arguing for the non-propositionality of hinges is not a mere exegetical or terminological exercise. Not only is it vital to Wittgenstein's solution to the problem of infinite regress, it also coheres with his unrelenting effort, throughout his philosophizing, to get rid of the 'propositional assumption'[30] that riddles epistemology, philosophy generally and the cognitive

---

[30] An expression I owe to Harrison (2013).

sciences. That is, the misguided belief that propositions are indispensable to our grasp of the world. Only by maintaining the non-propositionality of hinges can we do full justice to Wittgenstein's radical recognition that in the beginning is 'something animal' (OC §359; §475) – the deed, acting – and not inner beliefs or thoughts, not basic propositions:

> As if giving grounds did not come to an end sometime. But the end is not an ungrounded presupposition: it is an ungrounded way of acting. (OC §110)

> Ask, not: 'What goes on in us when we are certain that . . . ?' – but: How is 'the certainty that this is the case' manifested in human action? (PI, p. 225)

1.7 Certainty as Enactive

Some philosophers contend that the groundlessness of hinge certainties is grist to the sceptic's mill. Williams (2021a, 184), for instance: 'Why is hinge epistemology an *answer* to skepticism rather than skepticism by another name?' Indeed, as Pritchard (2012b, 71) rhetorically points out: 'from a skeptical point of view it is hard to see just what is so anti-skeptical about the claim that the structure of rational evaluation has, at its core, arational commitments. Isn't that just what the radical skeptic claims?' Pritchard elaborates on Williams's view of hinge epistemology in 2.3.

It may be hard to see, but there *is* a difference between the sceptic's and Wittgenstein's view of the absence of justification. The ungroundedness of hinge certainties is not – as the sceptic would have it – due to an epistemic failing; it is – as Wittgenstein shows – a logical necessity. And far from precluding knowledge, ungrounded hinge certainties enable it.

What traditional epistemology has taken to be basic propositions are in fact unreflective ways of acting, that can be heuristically formulated as rules of thinking or bounds of sense. What the sceptic must accept is that, as David Egan (2021, 582) nicely puts it: 'our practices go deeper than our reasons can reach.' Enactivism, broadly understood,[31] is the view that mentality is – as Daniel Hutto (2014, 281) puts it: 'rooted in engaged, embodied activity as opposed to detached forms of thought'; a view that favours 'the primacy of ways of acting over ways of thinking when it comes to understanding our basic psychological and epistemic situation'.

Norman Malcolm and G. H. von Wright were the first to engage substantively with *On Certainty*, and both understood Wittgenstein's notion of certainty as

---

[31] As opposed to, more narrowly, the movement founded by Varela, Thompson & Rosch (1991).

what we would today call 'enactivist'. Malcolm writes:

> When Wittgenstein says that the primitive form of the language-game with the word 'cause' is 'certainty', he does not mean that the child affirms in his mind the proposition that the other one certainly knocked him down, or that the child has a perception or intuitive awareness of the causal connection between his being crashed into and his falling down. No.... The 'certainty' he is talking about is a certainty in behavior, not a certainty in propositional thought. (Malcolm 1995a, 70)

Having quoted OC §253: 'At the foundation of well-founded belief lies unfounded belief' [sic][32], he writes:

> In our present example, the 'unfounded belief' would be our belief, or we would call it *certainty*, that people can and do suffer physical pain even without visible bodily damage. This belief or certainty is displayed in our actions and reactions. It is not the result of reasoning; it could be called 'instinctive'. (Malcolm 1995b, 96)

This 'certainty in behavior' is instinctive or 'animal' (OC §475) in the sense that, as Malcolm puts 'it is not the result of reasoning'; keeping in mind that this includes not only natural behaviour but also conditioned behaviour.[33]

As for von Wright, he speaks of the background as a non-propositional 'pre-knowledge'; in fact, a certainty in action:

> Considering the way language is taught and learned, the fragments of a world-picture underlying the uses of language are not originally and strictly *propositions* at all. The pre-knowledge is not propositional knowledge. But if this foundation is not propositional, what then *is* it? It is, one could say, a *praxis*. (von Wright 1982, 178)

Avrum Stroll similarly acknowledged that, for Wittgenstein,

> [B]elief at that level is not a matter of knowing various propositions to be true or a kind of intellectual grasping. Instead, it is embedded in habitual action, in such ordinary behavior as opening and closing doors. When I leave the house my unhesitating movements exhibit the certitude that the front door is there. The belief or certitude I have in that case is not a thought in any Fregean or mentalistic sense. (Stroll 1994, 173)

Marie McGinn speaks of a practical mastery of a system of judgements:

---

[32] The original translation reads: 'At the foundation of well-founded belief lies belief that is not founded.'

[33] Malcolm (1982, 79) speaks of instinctive in the 'primary' and 'secondary' senses of the word.

> The idea of a foundation in certain knowledge is replaced by the idea of a basis in practical mastery of a system of judgements which together determine our techniques for describing the world in language. ... Our conviction in [these judgements] is not properly conceived as epistemic certainty regarding the truth of empirical propositions, for which the question of justification must inevitably arise, but as the immediate exercise of our practical mastery of our techniques for describing the world, for which the question of justification makes no sense. (1989, 145–46)

In *Last Writings on the Philosophy of Psychology*, Wittgenstein notes: 'Don't think of being certain as a mental state, a kind of feeling, or some such thing. The important thing about certainty is the way one behaves' (LW II, p. 21). Certainty is enactive: it manifests itself in action; *in what we say, think, do*: '... the end is not certain propositions striking us immediately as true ... it is our *acting*, which lies at the bottom of the language-game' (OC §204). My certainty of having hands manifests itself in my using them to type these words or in my saying 'My hands are cold'. How is it then that Wittgenstein describes hinges as rules (OC §95, §98, §494) – indeed, rules that belong to 'the *scaffolding* of our thoughts' (OC §211); to 'the substratum of all [*our*] enquiring and asserting' (OC §162) – that is, grammatical rules? Can a hinge certainty be both a way of acting and a grammatical rule?

One answer to this is Wittgenstein's *enactive* notion of rules: '"following a rule" is a practice' (PI §202). A rule is an enabler; to follow a rule is not to make a judgement, but to *make a move*: 'A rule is best described as being like a garden path in which you are trained to walk, and which is convenient. You are taught arithmetic by a process of training, and this becomes one of the paths in which you walk' (AWL 155). When we learn rules, we do not learn a content but a technique, a skill, a mastery – how to proceed. In the *Remarks on the Foundations of Mathematics*, Wittgenstein notes the dispensability of propositions in arithmetic, stressing the similarity of calculating to gestures, and of the teaching of arithmetic to a training:

> Might we not do arithmetic without having the idea of uttering arithmetical *propositions,* and without ever having been struck by the similarity between a multiplication and a proposition?
>
> Should we not shake our heads, though, when someone shewed us a multiplication done wrong, as we do when someone tells us it is raining, if it is not raining? – Yes; and here is a point of connection. But we also make gestures to stop our dog, e.g., when he behaves as we do not wish.
>
> We are used to saying '2 times 2 is 4', and the verb 'is' makes this into a proposition, and apparently establishes a close kinship with everything that we call a 'proposition'. Whereas it is a matter only of a very superficial relationship. (RFM Appendix III, 4)

Another answer to the dual aspect of hinges is that it reflects the dual perspective from which Wittgenstein elucidates our basic certainty in *On Certainty*. One perspective might be called *epistemological*. Here, Wittgenstein seeks to elucidate the status of hinge certainty in our epistemic structures, and this is where we get the hinge metaphor; the bedrock; the background; the ground; the substratum, which depict it as foundational; as something solid, hardened, immovable, unmoving, anchored. Hinges are 'the substratum of all my enquiring and asserting' (OC §162); they 'form the foundation of all operating with thoughts (with language)' (OC §401). Our hinge certainties, then, do constitute a foundation, but one that differs from the norm in epistemology in that it is not constituted of things we *know*. The foundation is neither epistemic nor propositional; it is logical or grammatical.

The second perspective is *enactive*: here, Wittgenstein is describing *what it is like* to be basically certain – and the answer is that it is like an unreflective way of acting or attitude, a know-how or reflex action (like taking hold of my towel (OC §510)). My certainty that this is my friend DP standing in front of me manifests itself in my speaking to him without a moment's hesitation – that is, without first questioning and ascertaining that it is really him; that he really is a person or a human being; that human beings can speak; that human beings exist and so on.

In fact, from this perspective, our hinge certainties are ineffable. Wittgenstein makes clear that the utterance of a hinge outside a heuristic context makes no sense. Uttering a hinge, *qua* hinge, in the flow of ordinary discourse is to speak nonsense; it is to utter a rule where no reminder of the rule is needed. If I were to say to my doctor as I point to my aching hand: 'This is a hand', she would look at me perplexed. Why am I saying this? 'The background is lacking for [this] to be information' (OC §461). The information the doctor requires in order to relieve my pain is where my hand hurts: that this ∅ is a hand is the ineffable hinge upon which her helping me out of my misery revolves. Our shared certainty that this ∅ is a hand can only *show* itself in our normal *transaction* with my hand; it cannot *qua certainty* be meaningfully *said*. Articulating a hinge in the language game does not result in a display of certainty, but in a display of nonsense. It is perceived as queer; incomprehensible; a joke; a sign of madness (OC §553; §347; §463; §467). To utter a hinge certainty *within* the language-game invariably arrests the game. Conversely, think of the fluidity of the game poised on its invisible hinges: I let the doctor examine my hand while pointing to where it hurts and she decides it is fractured and will need a cast.

Of course, Wittgenstein and Moore do verbalise some of our certainties, but they do so in a heuristic context: their utterances are cases of 'mention' not 'use', and are not, therefore, subject to the nonsensicality to which they are subject when uttered in non-heuristic discourse.[34] Hinge certainties can be uttered in the study without this arresting the philosophical language-game. This is not because they become dubitable propositions when scrutinized in the pondered atmosphere of philosophical reflection, but because in the study their nature and status are being elucidated, and so they are *mentioned, not used*. On this point, see Pritchard's discussion of Williams's inferential contextualism (2.3).

Schönbaumsfeld (2016, 123n21; 120) not only questions the intelligibility of the view that certainty is both grammatical and a way of acting, she denies – *contra* McGinn (1989, 160), Moyal-Sharrock (2005) and Coliva (2010) – that certainty can be thought of as an *attitude* at all: 'in ordinary circumstances, I don't have any particular doxastic attitude towards my hands – I just use them' (2016, 122–23); in fact, 'it is misleading to speak of an "attitude" here at all' (2016, 123), doxastic or otherwise. I suggest that Schönbaumsfeld may have has too cognitive an understanding of 'attitude' – an understanding which overlooks the reflex-like nature of the diverse attitudinal metaphors used by Wittgenstein to describe hinge certainty: 'it is just like a direct taking hold of something, as I take hold of my towel without having doubts' (OC §510); 'it stands fast for me that' (e.g. OC §116, §125, §144; §151); an attitude – albeit a non-propositional one – of relying on (OC §509); of trust (OC §337); of 'staying in the saddle however much the facts bucked' (OC §616). These attitudinal stances of certainty reflect Wittgenstein's efforts to draw a crucial difference between traditional views of basic beliefs and his own enactive view:

> I want to say: it's not that on some points men know the truth with perfect certainty. No: perfect certainty is only a matter of their *attitude*. (OC §404; my emphasis)

Schönbaumsfeld's objection that hinges cannot be seen as both expressing rules of grammar and being a way of acting seems odd in that she herself takes them to be 'logical enabling conditions' (2016, 128) that reveal themselves in what we say and do (2016, 118). And inasmuch as she agrees that 'we can, for heuristic reasons, on occasion articulate the logical enabling conditions that make our epistemic practices possible' (2016, 122) – what is that if not articulating the rules of grammar that enable our basic ways of speaking and acting?

In opposition to our traditional conception of basic beliefs, Wittgenstein wants to make clear that basic certainty is an unreflective way of acting – 'It

---

[34] Or when overheard by someone unaware of the heuristic nature of the circumstances:

> I am sitting with a philosopher in the garden: he says again and again 'I know that that's a tree', pointing to a tree that is near us. Someone else arrives and hears this, and I tell him: 'This fellow isn't insane. We are only doing philosophy'. (OC §467)

is our *acting*, which lies at the bottom of the language-game' (OC §204) – not a tacit belief. The hinge certainty verbalised as: 'I have a body' reflects the disposition of a living creature which manifests itself in her *acting in the certainty of having a body*:[35] that is, she feeds, washes, scratches, dresses, photographs herself; she complains of having aches and pains; and she says things like 'I've got goosebumps all over' or 'I need to go to the gym.' Hinge certainty has the unhesitating fluidity of animal behaviour; it is not rational or irrational but *a*rational or animal:

> I want to conceive it ['this certainty' (OC §358)] as something that lies beyond being justified or unjustified; as it were, as something animal. (OC §359)

> I want to regard man here as an animal; as a primitive being to which one grants instinct but not ratiocination. As a creature in a primitive state. Any logic good enough for a primitive means of communication needs no apology from us. (OC §475)

And in order to do this – to regard man as an animal – Wittgenstein had to confront and uproot an overly reverent view of reason:

> Reason – I feel like saying – presents itself to us as the gauge *par excellence* against which everything that we do, all our language games, measure and judge themselves. – We may say: we are so exclusively preoccupied by contemplating a yardstick that we can't allow our gaze to *rest* on certain phenomena or patterns. We are used, as it were, to 'dismissing' these as irrational, as corresponding to a low state of intelligence, etc. The yardstick rivets our attention and keeps distancing us from these phenomena, as it were making us look beyond. (CE p. 389)

What *On Certainty* shows is that our distrust of the arational and our reliance on reason are excessive. Reason does not go all the way down: at the substratum of our thought is a logic that is animal – which means, it is nonreflective and, therefore, non-propositional. Exit infinite regress.

1.8 Hinge Certainties: A 'Reality-Soaked' Grammar

As we saw, the enactive and grammatical nature of hinges does away with the propositionality of hinges. Hinges are not propositions: 'the end is not an ungrounded presupposition: it is an ungrounded way of acting' (OC §110). Ways of acting[36] which, when formulated, do not express empirical propositions

---

[35] When asleep or unconscious, this certainty remains a disposition, but becomes occurrent in any normal use she makes of her body – for example, in her eating, running, her not attempting to walk through walls as if she were a disembodied ghost.

[36] Though mathematical hinges, for example, might not seem like 'ways of acting', recall:

but rules of grammar. That is, in Wittgenstein's sense, the *reality-soaked*[37] conditions of sense that manifest themselves in what we say and do. By 'reality-soaked' is meant *embedded in* or *conditioned by* reality – as opposed to *grounded in* or *justified by* reality: 'Indeed, doesn't it seem obvious that the possibility of a language-game is *conditioned* by certain facts?' (OC §617; my emphasis).

In his examination of the nature of our basic certainties, Wittgenstein does not limit himself to Moore's examples of things he indubitably 'knows': *On Certainty* contains about 300 examples of basic or hinge certainties. I have classified these into four kinds: 'linguistic', 'personal', 'local' and 'universal' hinges. These categories seem to me to best reflect and encompass the diverse examples evoked in *On Certainty*.

Hinge certainties are all foundational, but some are *universally*, others only *locally* so. All our certainties are unfounded, but some because they are instinctive, others because their acquisition is effected through sedimentation (implicit or explicit conditioning or repeated exposure). Whatever their origin, all hinges function as rules of grammar: they *condition* meaning and action. Being rules, they cannot be falsified but some can be abandoned, become obsolete, while others cannot (their rejection would 'drag everything with it and plunge it into chaos' (OC §613)).

The grammatical status of **linguistic** hinges (e.g., *'2+2 = 4'*, *'What the colour of human blood is called'*, *'The words composing this sentence are English'*, *'A is a physical object'* (OC §455, §340, §158, §36)) is obvious. Not themselves an object of analysis in *On Certainty*, they are mentioned as a benchmark against which the less obviously grammatical nature of the other three types of hinges is measured.[38]

Personal hinges (e.g., *'For months I have lived at address A'*, *'I am now sitting in a chair'*, *'I am in England'*, *'I have never been in Bulgaria'*, *'I have never been on the moon'*, *'I have just had lunch'*, *'The person opposite me is my old friend so and so'* (OC §70, §§552–53, §421, §269, §111, §659, §613)) have to do with our individual lives.

Local hinges (e.g., *'No one was ever on the moon'*, *'It isn't possible to get to the moon'*, *'The earth is round'*, *'Trains normally arrive in a railway station'* (OC §106, §106, §291, §339)) belong, or have belonged, to the world picture of a community of people at a given time. Some local hinges (e.g., 'It is possible to get to the moon') begin life as objects of knowledge or propositions (e.g., we

---

A rule is best described as being like a garden path in which you are trained to walk, and which is convenient. You are taught arithmetic by a process of training, and this becomes one of the paths in which you walk. (AWL 155)

[37] An expression I borrow from Bernard Harrison.   [38] See, e.g., (OC §448 & §657).

knew it is possible to get to the moon when the *Apollo 11* mission landed on the moon on 20 July 1969). However, it is not *qua* empirical propositions that they become hinge certainties, but by fusing into the foundations through repeated exposure, hardening, fossilization (e.g., 'This fact is fused into the foundations of our language-game' (OC §558)). Conversely, some hinges can be ousted from bedrock (e.g., 'No one was ever on the moon'), like rules that have become obsolete.[39] Not all hinges are susceptible of expulsion; it is impossible to dislodge from one's bedrock personal hinges such as 'I have a daughter', or local hinges such as 'Human beings have been to the moon', or any of our universal hinges.

Universal hinges are foundational for all normal human beings at any given time (e.g., *'I have forbears', 'If someone's head is cut off, the person will be dead and not live again', 'Trees do not gradually change into men and men into trees'* (OC §234, §274, §513). Wittgenstein speaks of the bedrock of our thoughts as consisting 'partly of sand, which now in one place now in another gets washed away, or deposited', but also 'partly of hard rock subject to *no alteration*' (OC §99; my emphasis). The hard rock that is subject to no alteration stands for some of our personal certainties (e.g., 'I have never been on the moon') as well as our universal certainties: those that 'underlie *all* questions and *all* thinking' (OC §415; my emphasis). 'Human beings express feelings' is such an example; so were we to meet a tribe of people brought up from early youth to give no expression of feeling of any kind, we could not see these people as human:

> 'These men would have nothing human about them.' Why? – We could not possibly make ourselves understood to them. Not even as we can to a dog. We could not find our feet with them. (Z 390)

That human beings express feeling is part of the 'substratum' of human thought (OC §161); it is one of those 'universal certainties' that logically or grammatically underpin anything any normal human being can say or think about other humans. Universal certainties are conditioned by very general facts of nature which importantly include 'the common behaviour of mankind ... the system of reference by means of which we interpret an unknown language' (PI 206) – by

---

[39] It may seem that because the hinge is ousted by my finding out something, it was susceptible of falsification. But as hinges are rules or ways of acting (depending on whether we are describing them from an epistemological or from an enactive perspective (see 1.7)), and therefore not susceptible of truth and falsity, their ousting is not due to falsification but to finding out that the rule is otiose. In the same way that when, for some empirical, practical or other reason, we decide to cancel a rule in a game or in a code of conduct, this doesn't make the rule susceptible of falsification. For a more detailed discussion of the processes by which some of our hinges become 'fixed' (and, conversely, 'unhinged'), see Moyal-Sharrock (2005, 104–16, 137–47).

which is meant any *human* language. Very general facts of nature – such as that we are creatures who inhabit and interact in a world peopled by other creatures; and (excepting pathological cases) acquire and use language, have and express feelings and emotions – *logically* condition the concepts or grammar of all normal human beings; the intelligibility of any human language.

Whereas very general facts of nature are objects of certainty for all humans, the facts that frame the various forms of human life are objects of certainty for only some humans, depending on culture, society, education, interest and so on. It will be a given for all human beings that people need to breathe air, eat, drink, sleep; that most can walk, feel pain, and use language; that they normally live in communities. But only for some will it be a given that there is a God, or that sacrifices should be performed, or that the future can be read in the entrails of a chicken.[40]

The last three sets of hinges may seem unlikely candidates for the role of grammatical rules, but it is precisely to Wittgenstein's credit that he uncovered the logical role played by what *appear* to be empirical and epistemic propositions. The status of a sentence is not determined by its appearance but by its use. For Wittgenstein: 'What belongs to grammar are all the conditions (the method) necessary ... for the understanding (of the sense)' (PG, p. 88): our hinge certainties are all part of this 'method' (OC §151).

1.9 Psychological Certainty

Of the many examples Wittgenstein gives of hinge certainties in *On Certainty*, there is a subgroup of personal hinges that, though present in *On Certainty*, is mostly addressed in his writings and lectures on philosophical psychology, the last of which – *Last Writings on the Philosophy of Psychology, vol. II* – is contemporaneous with the notes that make up *On Certainty*. These are *psychological* certainties.[41]

As is well known, Wittgenstein pointed out an asymmetry between first- and third-person psychological statements: 'The salient thing [about the psychological verb] is the asymmetry; "I think", unlike "he thinks", has no verification' (LPP 49); 'The truth is: it makes sense to say about other people that they doubt whether I am in pain; but not to say it about myself' (PI 246). The latter, unlike the former, are dependent on observation, and are thereby *constitutionally* open

---

[40] On universal and local moral hinge certainty, see Pleasants (2008) and O'Hara (2018).
[41] The mentions in *On Certainty*, of what can be called psychological certainties, are to our basic reliance on / certainty about our memory (cf. OC §§66, 201, 337, 345, 346, 416, 419, 497, 506, 632); to one's certainty of being in pain as the benchmark for basic, noncognitive certainty (cf. OC §§41, 178, 504); and to one's claim that someone else is in pain as cognitive (OC §555) or perhaps not (OC §563).

to uncertainty: '[The] characteristic [of psychological verbs] is this, that their third person but not their first person is stated on grounds of observation' (RPP I, 836; cf. also RPP II, 63). However, following relentless questioning and wavering; for example:

> The uncertainty of the ascription 'He's got a pain' might be called a constitutional certainty. (RPP I, 141; see also RPP II, 657)

> The *uncertainty* whether someone else ... is an (essential) trait of all these language-games. But this does not mean that everyone is hopelessly in doubt about what other people feel. (LW I, 877)

> Subjective and objective certainty.
>   Why do I want to say '2x2=4' is objectively certain, and 'This man is in pain' only subjectively? (LW II, p. 23)

> Need I be less certain that someone is suffering pain than that 12 x 12 = 144? (LW II, p. 92)

– Wittgenstein qualifies this asymmetry by challenging the *constitutional* uncertainty of third-person psychological sentences. He concedes that some third-person psychological certainties are not merely subjective; they are logically indubitable (that is of the same order as 'I am in pain' or '2 x 2 = 4'):

> Just try – in a real case – to doubt someone else's fear or pain. (PI 303)

> If we see someone falling into the flames and crying out, do we say to ourselves: 'there are of course two cases: ... '? Or if I see you here before me do I distinguish? Do you? *You can't!* That we do in certain cases, doesn't show that we do in all cases. (LPE 287; my emphasis)

> 'I can only guess at someone else's feelings' – does that really make sense when you see him badly wounded, for instance, and in dreadful pain? (LW I, 964)

> If I see someone writhing in pain with evident cause I do not think, all the same, his feelings are hidden from me. (LW II, 22)

> But of course it isn't true that we are never certain about the mental processes in someone else. In countless cases we are. (LW II, 94)

Psychological uncertainty about others turns out not to be pervasive. There are cases where we *cannot* be mistaken because there is no *logical* room for mistake, even in the case of third-person psychological certainties.[42] This, of course, bolsters Wittgenstein's noncognitive approach to mentality. The insight

---

[42] For a more elaborate discussion of psychological certainty, see Moyal-Sharrock (2007b).

that, in some cases, we are logically certain of what someone else is feeling makes the necessity of 'mindreading', or the positing of a default 'theory of mind', otiose.

The extraordinary thing about Wittgenstein's philosophising is that it is never behind the scenes. Because what we have of it is mostly in the form of notes or lectures, we see the work *in progress*. Though in no linear progression, we see the doubts, the confusion, the emerging clarity and the eureka moments. In the first section of this Element, we have followed him in his questioning of the primacy of knowledge and his bequeathing this primacy to certainty – a certainty from which he gradually peels off the epistemic veneer to find the spontaneity of the animal and the rigour of the rule. With this, he leaves epistemology transformed.

2 Hinge Commitments in Contemporary Epistemology

2.1 Introductory Remarks

In Section 1, we were introduced by Danièle Moyal-Sharrock to some of the main themes in *On Certainty* and the manner in which these themes intersect with the rest of Wittgenstein's work. Moyal-Sharrock then set out the case for thinking of our *hinge commitments* (or *hinge certainties,* as she prefers to call them) – this core notion that Wittgenstein introduces in *On Certainty* (albeit not with this terminology exactly) – along non-propositional lines. The goal of Section 2 is to offer an alternative perspective on these issues by considering some of the main ways in which *On Certainty* has been read in contemporary epistemology (excluding, of course, Moyal-Sharrock's own influential reading, which has already been covered). In doing so, we will get a sense of the tremendous impact this work has had, particularly with regard to thinking about the problem of radical scepticism.

Bringing hinge commitments into one's epistemology leads to a profoundly anti-foundationalist account of the structure of rational evaluation. Rather than our knowledge being ultimately supported by beliefs that enjoy a paradigmatic rational status (and hence function as something akin to 'unmoved movers' in the structure of rational evaluation), such as by being self-evident or incorrigible, the regress of reasons instead terminates, quite properly, with our optimal certainty in arational hinge commitments.[43] As we will see, although the *On Certainty*-inspired proposals in the contemporary literature that we will be looking at are fairly diverse in nature, what they share is the idea that our hinge commitments are contentful propositional commitments, albeit of a distinctive epistemic kind. In particular, while our hinge commitments are

---

[43] Here I diverge from Moyal-Sharrock's comments in this regard in Section 1, where she takes *On Certainty* to be offering a distinctive kind of foundationalism.

fundamentally rooted in action and also perform a rule-like role in our practices, this is held to be compatible with them being propositional commitments, such that there is a particular proposition that one is hinge committed to. This thus sets these views apart from the position considered in Section 1.

One important *caveat* to make before proceeding is to alert the reader to the fact that while all the figures we discuss treat hinge commitments as propositional commitments, they don't all agree on *which* propositional commitments count as hinge commitments. With this in mind, there will be cases where what counts as an example of a hinge commitment for one author does not count as an example of an hinge commitment for another author. Moreover, some of these proposals grant that there are putative hinge commitments ascribed to Wittgenstein that are lacking in content, but this is not because they are siding with a non-propositional reading. Rather their claim is that it was a mistake to regard these particular propositions as hinge commitments in the first place.

I just described these contemporary proposals as '*On Certainty*-inspired', and that leads me to a second point of qualification. This is that several of the main treatments of hinge commitments in the contemporary literature are not explicitly offered as interpretations of *On Certainty* but rather as proposals that merely draw inspiration from this work. This is, of course, in marked contrast to the kind of project described by Moyal-Sharrock in Section 1, which is overtly exegetical.[44]

2.2 Strawson's Naturalism

We will begin with the first major philosopher to offer a sustained engagement with *On Certainty*, Peter Strawson in his *Skepticism and Naturalism: Some Varieties*.[45] Like the other commentators we will be looking at, Strawson is particularly interested in how *On Certainty* can provide the resources to deal with the problem of radical scepticism.[46] He argues for a naturalistic reading in this regard, one that allies the later Wittgenstein with Hume.

---

[44] Inevitably, in any survey of this kind some interesting proposals will not be covered. I want to mention two in particular: McGinn (1989) and Schönbaumsfeld (2016). McGinn's view is significant both because she was one of the first to offer a sustained discussion of *On Certainty* and because she takes the line that our hinge commitments amount to a distinctive kind of non-inferential knowledge, a contention that she relates to similar proposals found in the work of Sellars and McDowell. For a useful overview of McGinn's position in this regard, see McGinn (2010). While space prevents me from discussing Schönbaumsfeld's proposal, I do offer some brief remarks about its main features in endnotes 72 and 77 (and her position is also discussed in Section 1). For two surveys of the contemporary epistemological literature on hinge commitments, see Pritchard (2011a, 2017a).

[45] See Strawson (1985, especially ch. 1). So far as I'm aware, the first book-length discussion of *On Certainty* is Morawetz (1979).

[46] This treatment of scepticism is a marked change from Strawson's (1959, 1966) previously transcendental response to scepticism, as he acknowledges.

The following passage is worth quoting (almost) in its entirety, as it usefully summarizes the main contours of Strawson's proposal:

> [*Hume and Wittgenstein*] have in common the view that our 'beliefs' in the existence of body and, to speak roughly, in the general reliability of induction are not grounded beliefs and at the same time are not open to serious doubt. They are ... outside our critical and rational competence in the sense that they define, or help to define, the area in which that competence is exercised. To attempt to confront the professional skeptical doubt with arguments in support of these beliefs is to show a total misunderstanding of the role they actually play in our belief-systems. The correct way with the professional skeptic is not to attempt to rebut it with argument, but to point out that it is idle, unreal, a pretense: and then the rebutting arguments will appear as equally idle; the reasons produced in those arguments to justify induction or belief in the existence of body are not, and do not become, *our* reasons for these beliefs; there is no such thing as *the reasons for which we hold* these beliefs. We simply cannot help accepting them as defining the areas within which the questions come up of what beliefs we should rationally hold on such-and-such a matter. (Strawson 1985, 21)

There is a lot to unpack here, but we can discern the main contours of Strawson's reasoning. To begin with, the hinge commitments that Strawson are concerned with (although he doesn't use this terminology) are primarily anti-sceptical claims about the existence of an external world ('existence of body') and of the general reliability of induction. In what follows, we will focus on the former, given its prominence in contemporary epistemology. Strawson is interpreting Wittgenstein as claiming that our hinge commitments, so construed, are the product of our natures rather than reason. As such, they are groundless commitments that we simply cannot help but have. Accordingly, it is held to follow that doubt of them, while not senseless, is nonetheless idle, as it is simply impossible, given our natures.[47] Strawson concludes that radical scepticism, since it involves treating such claims as open to doubt, rests on a misunderstanding. Indeed, according to Strawson, traditional *anti*-scepticism, which attempts to rebut radical scepticism, rests on the same misunderstanding. The correct respond to scepticism is rather to ignore it.

It is certainly true that Wittgenstein emphasises the brute, arational nature of our hinge commitments. Rather than being due to reason, as we might antecedently imagine, they constitute instead a visceral kind of certainty, one that is

---

[47] At least, he suggests that they cannot be subject to 'serious' doubt anyway, but it is clear from the context that the relevant contrast in play here is not with a *bona fide* type of doubt of a less serious kind, but rather with a non-genuine kind of doubt that is a mere 'pretense' (as when a philosopher presents themselves as doubting these claims, when in fact, according to Strawson, they could do no such thing).

'animal', 'primitive' (e.g., OC §395, §475). Relatedly, Wittgenstein also emphasises the primacy of action in this regard, a topic that was covered extensively in Section 1. Indeed, he approvingly quotes Goethe in this respect: 'In the beginning was the deed' (OC §396). Wittgenstein would thus agree that doubt of our hinge commitments would be either a pretense, and so not genuine at all, or else genuine but then of a kind that we could make no sense of it. As he notes at a number of places, if we came across someone who genuinely doubted a hinge commitment, we would treat that person as mentally disturbed, and hence try to make sense of their doubt in terms of causes rather than reasons (has the person had a bump on the head?) (e.g., OC §§71–75).

While there are these surface agreements between Strawson's proposal and Wittgenstein's remarks in *On Certainty*, however, there are also fundamental differences. The most significant for our current purposes is that while Wittgenstein makes these naturalistic claims about our hinge commitments, they do not play any load-bearing role in his response to radical scepticism. What carries the load is rather the diagnostic story that he offers about the structure of rational evaluation (which we will come to presently). I would also add a further fundamental difference (though this is more controversial), which is that, as I read *On Certainty* at least, Wittgenstein doesn't regard philosophical claims like 'There is an external world' as being hinge commitments at all, but rather treats them simply as nonsense (as occurs when language 'goes on holiday', to use his famous metaphor from the *Philosophical Investigations*). (PI §38) For Wittgenstein, our hinge commitments are not theoretical in nature, but rather fundamental nodes of commonsense (this is a point I will be returning to).[48]

That Wittgenstein's response to radical scepticism is not naturalistic is fortunate, as such a line gains no purchase at all on the contemporary problem of radical scepticism.[49] The reason for this is that this problem is formulated as a *paradox* rather than as a position.[50] That is, the putative problem of radical

---

[48] Strawson recognizes that Wittgenstein's conception of our basic 'natural' commitments is broader than Hume's, in that it takes in these everyday commonsense claims (he writes that Wittgenstein's naturalism is as a consequence of a 'social' kind), but he also (mistakenly in my view) reads Wittgenstein as in addition treating the Humean claims as hinge commitments as well. It is quite common among contemporary epistemological work to treat a claim like 'There is an external world' as a hinge commitment. See, for example, Wright (2004b) or Coliva (2015). Like Williams (2004, 2018), however, I think this is a misreading of the first notebook of *On Certainty* (§§1–65), which I take to be making the case that such statements are simply nonsense. See Pritchard (2015, part 2, 2022b).

[49] I am here disagreeing with Moyal-Sharrock's remarks in this regard in 1.5, as she clearly does hold that this naturalistic point has a bearing on the radical sceptical paradox.

[50] The contention that we should think of the contemporary problem of radical scepticism in this fashion is usually credited to Stroud (1984). For further discussion of the contemporary debate regarding radical scepticism, see Coliva & Pritchard (2022).

scepticism is meant to consist in a fundamental tension within our own natural ways of thinking about knowledge, such that there is no way of resolving this paradox that does not involve large-scale revisionism of our ordinary epistemic concepts. So construed, radical scepticism does not incorporate any claim to the effect that there is a radical sceptical conclusion that can coherently be endorsed. Accordingly, the problem posed by this paradox survives the point that radical scepticism is incoherent as a position.

It will be useful at this juncture to flesh out what this paradox is supposed to be. The putative tension is between the following three claims:

The Radical Sceptical Paradox
(1) We have lots of everyday knowledge.
(2) We cannot know the denials of radical sceptical hypotheses.
(3) The closure principle.

The first claim captures our ordinary anti-sceptical epistemic commitments. As regards the second claim, the suggestion isn't that in our ordinary epistemic practices we routinely consider radical sceptical scenarios. Even so, however, the thought is that we can grasp what such scenarios involve, not least from ratcheting-up from more mundane error-possibilities of a kind that we do routinely encounter in everyday life. (Indeed, that we do grasp such scenarios, or at least seem to, is suggested by their prevalence in some non-philosophical contexts, such as in literature or the movies.) Since radical sceptical scenarios call one's beliefs into question en masse, so it seems that there cannot be a non-bootstrapping way of knowing that they are false.

On the face of it, of course, there is no obvious tension between the idea that we know lots of mundane facts about cabbages and kings and yet fail to know the denials of radical sceptical hypotheses. But this is where the closure principle comes into play. In its most plausible form, this principle states that where one undertakes competent deductions from one's knowledge, and forms a belief on this basis, then the resulting belief amounts to knowledge.[51] So if I know that Paris is the capital of France, and competently deduce from this knowledge that Madrid is not the capital of France, then I know that Madrid is not the capital of France. Such a principle seems to be highly intuitive and also, relatedly, embedded within our ordinary epistemic practices. The closure principle is usually benign, but generates quite startling results when we plug-in

---

[51] Since this is a diachronic principle, then strictly speaking we should also add the requirement that the knowledge of the antecedent proposition is retained throughout the competent deduction (though for simplicity we will take this complication for granted in what follows). This version of closure is essentially that put forward by Williamson (2000, 117) and Hawthorne (2005, 29).

radical sceptical scenarios.[52] The problem is that most of our everyday beliefs, such as that one has hands, are unhesitatingly regarded as amounting to knowledge. But if they are knowledge, then it seems that one can use the closure principle to competently deduce the denial of radical sceptical hypotheses (if one had hands, then one cannot be a handless brain-in-a-vat, for example).

We thus get the fundamental sceptical tension that was advertised. Moreover, this tension appears to be arising within our ordinary ways of thinking about knowledge, as each claim, at least when taken in isolation, seems to be something that we would naturally endorse. Insofar as these three claims really are in tension as the radical sceptic maintains, however, then it follows that the only way out of the paradox is to reject at least one of them, and that means embracing the radical revisionism of our ordinary epistemic practices that this implies. Radical scepticism *qua* position would involve the rejection of the first claim, but notice that radical scepticism *qua* paradox does not involve the rejection of *any* of these claims. In particular, as with any genuine philosophical paradox, the one proposing the puzzle merely needs to note the fundamental tension that exists within our own natural ways of thinking within the relevant domain and nothing more. Indeed, someone who was presenting the problem of radical scepticism *qua* paradox would be wise to emphasise the absurdity of denying the radical sceptical horn of the trilemma, just as denying either of the other two horns would also be absurd.

With the foregoing in mind, it is entirely irrelevant to the contemporary version of the problem of radical scepticism to note that one is unable to coherently embrace the radical sceptical conclusion. Such a point fails to engage with the problem of radical scepticism *qua* paradox; in fact, it is something that the purveyor of the radical sceptical paradox can herself endorse. What we require is instead a *diagnosis* of where the radical sceptical paradox goes awry, where this means either an explanation of why one of the revisionary options is palatable or, ideally, an explanation of why this ostensible paradox is in fact illusory.[53] Wittgenstein's line in *On Certainty*, as we will see, is very much along the latter lines, in keeping with his more general approach to apparently deep philosophical problems.

---

[52] It has been suggested that such a principle can undermine our (putative) everyday knowledge even when local error-possibilities are in play. See, for example, Dretske (1970), bearing in mind that he was discussing a precursor of our current formulation of the closure principle (though his point, if it held, should equally apply to our formulation). As I argue in Pritchard (2010b, 2012a, 2022c), however, this is based on an impoverished conception of the rational basis for our everyday beliefs.

[53] See Pritchard (2015a, part 1) for further discussion of these two styles of anti-scepticism as, respectively, overriding and undercutting responses. See also Williams (1991, ch. 1) and Cassam (2007, ch. 1) for discussion of similar distinctions between kinds of anti-sceptical proposal.

It is an interesting question why Strawson failed to recognise this point himself, given his otherwise acute philosophical sensibilities. One reason might be that the framing of the radical sceptical problem as a paradox was not particularly explicit in the literature at the time he was writing. A related issue in this respect is the extent to which his eagerness to relate Wittgenstein's anti-sceptical line to Hume's naturalistic response to scepticism blinded him to the fact that these philosophers were effectively engaging with very different sceptical problems. The radical sceptic that Hume is directing his naturalism against was the Pyrrhonian sceptic, and of course this is an embodied scepticism, scepticism as a position.[54] It is thus entirely relevant for Hume to point out that such scepticism cannot be coherently lived because of the necessity of certain anti-sceptical commitments. But such a line is completely ineffective, as we have seen, if we direct it against radical scepticism *qua* paradox.[55]

2.3 Williams's Inferential Contextualism

In his widely influential book, *Unnatural Doubts: Epistemological Realism and the Basis of Scepticism*, Michael Williams (1991) offers an important account of hinge commitments – or 'methodological necessities', as he calls them (Williams 1991, 123) – and their relevance to radical scepticism. Williams is explicit that he takes his proposal to be inspired by *On Certainty* rather than being completely faithful to it. In any case, the resulting position is a form of contextualism, albeit of a very different kind to the attributor contextualism that is familiar from contemporary epistemology.[56] Elsewhere I have called Williams's proposal *inferential contextualism*, on the grounds that it regards the inferential structure in play in our rational practices as determined by context, such that what counts as a good reason for what can change quite dramatically in response to contextual factors.[57]

---

[54] Note that although Wittgenstein's target is radical scepticism as a paradox, there are undoubted Pyrrhonian influences on his work (just as there also clear Pyrrhonian influences on Hume's anti-scepticism, even despite it being explicitly opposed to this form of scepticism – see also endnote 56). For further discussion of these influences, see Sluga (2004), and Pritchard (2019a, 2019b, *forthcomingb*).

[55] I discuss this point (including the exegetical issues surrounding Hume's oddly Pyrrhonian response to Pyrrhonian scepticism), and Strawson's anti-scepticism more generally, in more detail in Pritchard (*forthcomingd*). For further discussion of the contrasts between Humean and Wittgensteinian anti-scepticism specifically, see Pritchard (2024d). For some useful critical treatments of Strawson's (1985) naturalistic response to radical scepticism, see Putnam (1998, cf. Strawson 1998b), Sosa (1998, cf. Strawson 1998a), Stern (2003), and Callanan (2011).

[56] For some of the key texts on attributer contextualism, see Lewis (1996), DeRose (1996), and Cohen (1999).

[57] See especially Pritchard (2002), which critically compares and contrasts inferential and attributer versions of contextualism.

Before we get to Williams's distinctive brand of contextualism, however, it will be useful to map out some of the core features of his proposal that lead him to develop this view. According to Williams, Wittgenstein is responding to the particular challenge that is posed by radical scepticism *qua* paradox. Williams argues, correctly in my opinion, that Wittgenstein is offering a diagnostic story about the structure of rational evaluation that undercuts the putative paradox posed by radical scepticism. In particular, what Wittgenstein is trying to get us to see is the incoherence of universal rational evaluations – that is, rational evaluations that bring all of our commitments under scrutiny at once.

As we saw in 2.2, it is possible to present the radical sceptical paradox such that it seems to rest only on uncontentious features of our ordinary epistemic practices. In particular, while it is true that radical sceptical doubts do not normally arise in ordinary epistemic contexts, it seems that there is no in principle barrier to us extending the scope of our rational evaluations without limit in response to challenges, such that we could potentially rationally evaluate our entire worldview. If this were correct, then that would suffice to put the radical sceptical paradox on a firm footing, since it would show that there are deep tensions in our natural ways of thinking about our epistemic concepts, of a kind that entails contradictions. The radical sceptic isn't introducing anything new but is rather merely drawing out how our ordinary epistemic concepts, at least when employed in thorough-going ways, generate paradox.

In contrast, Williams treats Wittgenstein as making vivid how the very idea of universal rational evaluations is in fact completely alien to our ordinary epistemic practices. This is because those practices presuppose one's arational certainty in one's hinge commitments. In particular, the idea is that it is not an incidental feature of our epistemic practices that they function in this way, but is rather built into the very idea of what it means for there to be a rational practice. As Wittgenstein emphasises at a number of junctures, the point he is making is one of 'logic' (e.g., OC §342). If that's right, then what the radical sceptic is doing in introducing such radical doubt is not applying our ordinary epistemic practices in a purified fashion, but in fact trading on a conception of an epistemic practice that is entirely divorced from our everyday practices and which is independently implausible. It follows that the putative radical sceptical paradox is shown to be illusory, since it is motivated by dubious theoretical claims masquerading as commonsense. Our ordinary epistemic practices are thus entirely in order as they are (at least with regard to the threat of radical scepticism at any rate).

This is a considerable advance on Strawson's naturalism, as we now have a concrete way of understanding how hinge commitments can be employed to block the radical sceptical paradox. Unfortunately, other features of Williams's view are less compelling. Williams argues that once we embrace hinge commitments, and thereby discard the idea of universal rational evaluations, we are led to reject a particular metaphysical view about the objects of epistemological study. Williams calls this faulty metaphysical thesis *epistemological realism*, which is the claim that a proposition can have an inherent epistemic status in virtue of its content alone. In particular, Williams is especially interested in the idea, familiar to traditional foundationalism, that propositions concerning the 'inner' realm of one's own mind (e.g., regarding one's current mental states) have a privileged epistemic status relative to propositions concerning the 'outer' realm of an empirical world (e.g., regarding one's immediate environment). This is what Williams refers to as *epistemic priority*.

The thought is that beliefs regarding this inner realm can enjoy a privileged epistemic status simply in virtue of what they are about. In contrast, beliefs about the empirical world cannot enjoy a privileged epistemic status, where this again follows from their content. The upshot is that the inferential structure concerning these two classes of claims must inevitably be such that beliefs about the inner realm of the mind are epistemically more basic than beliefs about the empirical world. Indeed, Williams argues that it is from this picture that we get the foundationalist idea that beliefs about the inner realm have an intrinsic epistemic authority that allows them to be known non-inferentially, while beliefs about the world can only be known inferentially, drawing in the process from the base class. So, for example, on traditional foundationalist views rationally grounded empirical knowledge that there is chair in front of one must be based on an inference from one's beliefs about one's mental states (e.g., regarding one's experiences as of there being a chair before one).

Williams takes hinge epistemology to be opposed to epistemological realism, and this is where his inferential contextualism comes in. Williams argues that once we embrace hinge commitments, then what counts as a reason for what can vary with context. Just as moving the hinges on a door can lead to the door opening in a different direction, so any change in one's hinge commitments can alter what can count as a reason for what. Moreover, Williams is quite explicit that changes in context can change one's hinge commitments. In order to determine the epistemic status of a given belief it is thus vital to first determine what contextual parameters are in play, since otherwise a crucial ingredient in determining epistemic status is lacking:

> ... the epistemic status of a given proposition is liable to shift with situational, disciplinary and other contextually variable factors: ... independently of such influences, a proposition has no epistemic status whatsoever. (Williams 1991, 119)

In particular, Williams argues that we should reject epistemic priority and thereby allow that in some contexts (as part of a psychological investigation, say) it can be entirely appropriate to reason from claims about the 'outer' realm of the external world to claims about the 'inner' realm of someone's mental states.[58]

One feature of Williams's view that is problematic is his conception of hinge commitments. The purpose of the hinge metaphor for Wittgenstein is that something must stand fast (the arational certainty) in order for something else to function (rational evaluation). The point is that this hinge certainty performs a framework role in our rational practices by enabling rational evaluations to occur (which is also why the hinge must itself be arational, as there is no way to rationally evaluate it on this picture). This is just one metaphor that Wittgenstein uses in this regard, but it is the one that has stuck with commentators. Other metaphors he uses to describe our arational hinge certainty include 'scaffolding', 'inherited background' and the 'riverbed' of our system of rational evaluation. (OC §211, §94, §§401–3; §§96–99) Wittgenstein also talks of our hinge certainty as a 'foundation' of this system too, but he is quite explicit that it is not a foundation in the way that traditional foundationalism might imagine (i.e., in the epistemic 'unmoved mover' sense). He remarks that it is not that the foundation walls are carrying the house but rather that the whole house (i.e., one's worldpicture) is supporting the foundations (OC §§246–48).

The relevance of these other metaphors is that they reinforce the idea that what makes the hinge metaphor apt is merely that our hinge certainty is required to be in place for our system of rational evaluation to occur – that is, that it plays a framework role. Williams takes the hinge metaphor in a different direction, however. For as he notes, one can move one's hinges and when one does so the door will turn in different ways. So construed, the hinge metaphor implies a kind of optionality. That is to say, while it might always be essential that we have hinge commitments, it can be to a certain extent up to us which hinge commitments we elect to endorse. With this in mind, Williams imagines his hinge commitments being such that they are determined by, for example, what kinds of inquiries we choose to undertake, such that we can change our hinge commitments at will simply by changing our inquiries. So, for instance, when doing history it might be necessary to endorse hinge commitments regarding,

---

[58] I argue in Pritchard (2015a, part 2, 2018d) that it is a mistake to think that Wittgenstein's argument against universal rational evaluations has a bearing on an issue like epistemic priority. In particular, I argue that there are two logically distinct formulations of the radical sceptical paradox, one that trades on the closure principle and a second formulation that turns on an entirely different epistemic principle known as underdetermination. Issues about epistemic priority concern this latter formulation of the radical sceptical paradox, while the Wittgensteinian line only engages with the former formulation.

say, the general veracity of certain types of historical documentation that wouldn't be appropriate in other contexts:

> For a subject like history, there is more to method than abstract procedural rules. This is because the exclusion of certain questions (about the existence of the Earth, the complete and total unreliability of documentary evidence, etc.) amounts to the acceptance of substantial factual commitments. These commitments, which must be accepted, if what we understand by historical inquiry at all, have the status, relative to that form of inquiry, of *methodological necessities*. (Williams 1991, 123)

This is not how Wittgenstein was conceiving of our hinge commitments, however, so I think this is a case where a commentator has been misled by a metaphor. On the contrary, Wittgenstein is emphatic about how we have no direct control over our hinge commitments. This is one of the points that Strawson got right earlier: the primitive, animal nature of this commitment.

More generally, I think the wider point that Williams misses is that while he emphasises the heterogeneous nature of our hinge commitments, claiming that there are multiple types playing very different roles in our epistemic practices, for Wittgenstein our hinge commitments have a common source. For although Wittgenstein does describe lots of different kinds of proposition that play this hinge role, his primary contention is not about these hinge commitments to specific propositions at all but rather concerns an overarching arational certainty that we need to have in our worldview. This is what I have elsewhere termed the *über hinge commitment*, which involves an arational commitment to the general veracity of one's worldview. As Wittgenstein puts it:

> ... I did not get my picture of the world by satisfying myself of its correctness; nor do I have it because I am satisfied of its correctness. No: it is the inherited background against which I distinguish between true and false. (OC §94)

It is this über hinge certainty that needs to be in place in order for a child to acquire a worldview and thereby enter into the space of reasons at all. Here is Wittgenstein:

> The child learns by believing the adult. Doubt comes after belief. (OC §160)

To lack the über hinge commitment is to be unable to acquire the worldview and thereby undertake rational evaluations. It is this overarching certainty that is manifest in our actions and which is by its nature arational, given the framework role that it places in our epistemic practices.

The über hinge commitment will also manifest itself in hinge commitments to specific propositions where those propositions are so fundamental to one's worldview that a doubt here would call the über hinge commitment into question and hence 'drag everything with it and plunge it into chaos' (OC §613). Our hinge commitments to specific propositions – such as that (in normal circumstances) one has hands (e.g., OC §1), what one's name is (OC §425), and the language that one is speaking (OC §158) – are thus manifestations of our über hinge commitment.

Understanding this feature of our hinge commitments explains why our hinge commitments aren't such a disparate bunch after all, as they in fact all stand in a specific relationship to the über hinge commitment. Moreover, it also explains why our specific hinge commitments have the features that they do. It might antecedently be puzzling that one's certainty in one's hands is essentially arational, much less that it plays some sort of scaffolding or framework role in one's epistemic practices, but this becomes much less puzzling when we understand how it is essentially a manifestation of the arational über hinge commitment. But the key point for our current purposes is that so construed our hinge commitments are not optional in the way that Williams imagines, such that one can elect to change them at will (such as by simply changing one's direction of inquiry), much less are they theoretical claims (as might be applicable to the methodological necessities of a particular discipline).

This doesn't mean that one's hinge commitments to specific propositions cannot change, as obviously they do, but it does impose restrictions on how this might occur. For one thing, this will not happen as the direct result of rational processes, as this certainty is not grounded on reasons. But that doesn't entail that the processes by which they change are non-rational. For example, take one's hinge commitment, in normal circumstances, to having hands. If one were in suitably abnormal conditions, such as waking up in hospital after an explosion, then it might make perfect sense to wonder whether one has hands and, indeed, to take one's sight of one's hands as providing a rational basis for believing this. What such a case illustrates is that which specific hinge commitments manifest the über hinge commitment will change as circumstances change and, with them, one's wider non-hinge beliefs (which, since they are grounded in reasons, will usually be responsive to reasons). This is part of the point of Wittgenstein's river-bed analogy noted earlier, in that what can be at one time part of the river-bank (i.e., a manifestation of one's über hinge commitment) can be at another time part of the river (i.e., an ordinary empirical belief).[59] The kind of change that Wittgenstein is envisaging in

---

[59] This is one of the reasons why I depart from most other contemporary commentators in describing our hinge certainties as *hinge commitments* rather than as *hinge propositions*. This is because the particular proposition that is functioning as the hinge is not what is important – indeed, in different circumstances, as we've just seen, it might no longer function as a hinge – but rather the distinctive kind of certainty that we have to this proposition, one that manifests our overarching über hinge certainty.

our hinge commitments is not what Williams has in mind, however, as there is nothing optional about this process at all. Moreover, our hinge commitments are never theoretical claims as Williams allows but rather the fundamental nodes of commonsense that lie at the heart of our worldview.

Williams's brand of contextualism is thus not entailed by endorsing hinge commitments and hence rejecting the coherence of universal rational evaluations. This is fortunate, as Williams's contextualism leads him to make some important concessions to the radical sceptic. Consider this passage:

> The sceptic takes himself to have discovered, under the conditions of philosophical reflection, that knowledge of the world is impossible. But in fact, the most he has discovered is that knowledge of the world is *impossible under the conditions of philosophical reflection*. (Williams 1991, 130)

Just as attributor contextualism usually concedes that the radical sceptic asserts truths relative to their specific context of ascription, so Williams ends up granting that there is a coherent context of inquiry in which the radical sceptic, employing the hinge commitment of epistemological realism, ends up demonstrating the truth of radical scepticism (albeit only in a context-bound way). Once one goes down the road of inferential contextualism, then a concession of this kind becomes inevitable, since what would prevent the radical sceptic from embracing their own distinctive set of hinge commitments that would licence their unusual line of inquiry?

Rather than concede this point to the radical sceptic, however, I think it is far preferable to stick with Williams's original diagnostic treatment of radical scepticism as attempting to do something that is fundamentally incoherent (while passing this off as merely appealing to our commonsense conception of our epistemic practices). If we take that point seriously, then there simply is no radical sceptical context of inquiry, as the falsity of its imagined methodological necessities rules it out in advance. More generally, we should jettison the idea of hinge commitments as being variable in the manner that Williams proposes and instead take seriously their essentially visceral nature.[60]

2.4 Wright on Entitlement

One interesting feature of Williams's proposal is that he departs from most contemporary epistemologists in arguing that our hinge commitments amount to knowledge, even despite their lack of rational support.[61] His overarching

---

[60] I offer a more detailed critique of Williams's inferential contextualist proposal in Pritchard (2018d).
[61] See, for example, Williams (2018, 384 & ff.). McGinn (1989) takes a similar line – see endnote 44.

thought seems to be that so long as one's hinge commitments are true, then their hinge status ought to suffice to ensure that they are reasonable commitments to have and hence they can amount to knowledge. Williams also argues that Wittgenstein was committed to this claim, due to some of his remarks where he describes everyday certainties as being known (e.g., that other human beings have blood). (OC §341) I think this last point is based on a misreading of *On Certainty*, as I will explain below – not every certainty that Wittgenstein discusses in this work is a hinge certainty. But the idea that our hinge commitments might amount to knowledge also features in the next proposal that we will look at, which is due to Crispin Wright. Significantly, however, Wright offers an intriguing account of how our arational hinge commitments might enjoy this epistemic status.

Wright reads Wittgenstein in *On Certainty* as conceding to the radical sceptic that we are subject to a deep cognitive limitation, whereby there are presuppositions of our system of beliefs that cannot be themselves rationally grounded due to their presuppositional nature on pain of circularity. Wright thus understands the notion of a hinge commitments as a response to this cognitive limitation that the radical sceptic exposes. If it really is the case that we are required to have these presuppositional hinge commitments, then we can argue that such commitments must be reasonable even if they are not supported by rational support.

We can see the main moving parts of the negative component of Wright's proposal at work in this passage:

> I suggest that the principal message of *On Certainty* is that scepticism embodies an insight which Moore missed: the insight that to be a rational agent, reflectively pursuing any form of cognitive enquiry, means placing trust in suppositions which – at least on the occasion – are not themselves the fruits of such enquiry and are therefore not known. (Wright 2004a, 305)

As Wright puts it, radical scepticism incorporates an 'insight' about our cognitive limitations, one that turns on the fact that we are unable to rationally ground the 'suppositions' that are required for our enquiries. We are thus faced with a situation whereby we are obliged to simply trust these presuppositions in our inquiries, as they cannot be known.

The positive part of Wright's proposal is the ingenious suggestion that there might be a kind of epistemic support that can apply even to rationally groundless suppositions. This is the notion of *entitlement*:

> Trusting without evidence can still be rational or not. Entitlements are *warrants to trust* .... (Wright 2004b, 204)[62]

---

[62] It is important to note that Wright's notion of entitlement is not the same as that defended under the same name by Burge (1993, 2003).

The basic idea behind Wright's entitlement proposal is that where a commitment is required in order for one to be a rational agent at all – and where there are no specific reasons to doubt the proposition involved in this commitment (which there obviously won't be in the case of hinge commitments) – then one is entitled to trust this commitment. In short, trusting is in these conditions reasonable, even if it is not supported by reasons that indicate the truth of what is being presupposed in the target commitment. It will be useful to quote the following passage in full, as it offers a useful summary of Wright's positive proposal:

> [*The moral* . . .] to be taken from *On Certainty* is that the concept of warranted belief only gets substance within a framework in which it is recognised that all rational thought and agency involves ineliminable elements of blind trust. Since rational thought and agency are not an optional aspect of our lives, we are entitled – save when there is specific evidence to the contrary – to make the presuppositions that need to be made in living out our conception of the kind of world we inhabit and the kinds of cognitive powers we possess.
>
> To be entitled to accept a proposition in this way, of course, has no direct connection with the likelihood of its truth. We are rationally entitled to proceed on a basis of trust merely because (or when) there is no extant reason to believe it is misplaced and because, unless we do so, we cannot proceed at all. An epistemological standpoint which falls back on a conception of entitlement of this kind for the last word against scepticism needs its own version of (what is sometimes called) the Serenity Prayer: in ordinary enquiry, we must hope to be granted the discipline to take responsibility for what we can be responsible, the trust to accept what we must merely presuppose, and the wisdom to know the difference. (Wright 2004*a*, 305)

One point that should be emphasised about Wright's notion of entitlement is that it is not a purely pragmatic notion, even though it is also not fully epistemic (or, at least, not epistemic in a straightforward way). Wright is not claiming that we should embrace our hinge commitments because they are useful, even though rationally groundless. Rather, his contention is that if we are rational subjects – of a kind that undertake enquiries, form beliefs, engage in reasoning and so forth – then we are obliged to embrace our hinge commitments, even though they are rationally groundless. The thought is thus that our hinge commitments are the kind of commitments that rational subjects will have, which is why although they are rationally groundless they are nonetheless reasonable presuppositions to have, even from a purely epistemic point of view.

In construing our hinge commitments in this strategic fashion, Wright is led to think of hinge commitments along very specific lines. Hinge commitments for him are the presuppositions that one is rationally obliged to have if one is to undertake certain kinds of fundamental inquiries. The kinds of claims that he conceives of as hinge commitments thus include statements like 'There is an external world', 'There are other minds', 'The world did not come into existence moments ago', and 'There are regularities present in nature'. These are very different to the paradigmatic examples of hinge commitments that Wittgenstein gives, which as we've noted are core commonsense nodes of one's worldpicture rather than general theoretical claims of this kind. (Indeed, as I also noted earlier, Wittgenstein doesn't regard a statement like 'There is an external world' as a hinge commitment at all, since it is simply nonsense.)

By arguing that our hinge commitments can enjoy entitlements, Wright thus finds a way to allow them to amount to knowledge even while lacking rational support. That is, a true belief that enjoys the epistemic standing of an entitlement can amount to knowledge in virtue of that alone. Wright's concern to show that our hinge commitments can be known stems from his desire to retain the closure principle. Interestingly, however, the version of the closure principle that Wright wants to preserve is not the diachronic formulation we offered earlier. This was competent deduction closure, which we can express as follows:

Competent Deduction Closure
If one knows that p, and one undertakes a competent deduction from this knowledge, and forms a belief that q on this basis (while retaining one's knowledge that p throughout), then one knows that q.

The closure principle that Wright has in mind, in contrast, is instead a much simpler synchronic formulation that demands only that knowledge is closed under known entailments. Call this simple closure:

Simple Closure
If one knows that p, and knows that p entails q, then one also knows that q.

We noted earlier that the version of the radical sceptical paradox that primarily concerns us trades on a closure-style principle, and we offered competent deduction closure as the relevant formulation, given that it is the most compelling way to understand this principle. By putting the two principles side-by-side, we can easily see why this formulation is preferable. Imagine, for example, someone who knows that p and knows that p entails q, but who forms a belief that q on a basis that has nothing whatever to do with either instance of knowledge. Perhaps, for example, they know that the murderer is the person with access to the basement and that this entails that Jones is the murderer (since only he had access to the basement), but their belief that Jones is the murderer is solely the result of an irrational prejudice towards Jones (and so unconnected to this other knowledge). We would thus have a counterexample to simple closure, as the subject would lack knowledge of the entailed proposition even despite their knowledge of the entailing proposition and the entailment. In contrast, this sort of scenario is excluded by competent deduction closure, given that the belief in the entailed proposition needs to be based on the competent deduction. Accordingly, if we want to capture the radical sceptical paradox in its strongest form, then we need to appeal to competent deduction closure rather than simple closure.

Nonetheless, Wright's main concern with showing that our hinge commitments can amount to knowledge is to preserve simple closure. In particular, his worry is that if we don't have knowledge of our hinge commitments, then there will be straightforward counterexamples to simple closure. Consider, for example, one of Wright's putative hinge commitments, that the world didn't come into existence moments ago. There are lots of propositions that we take ourselves to know which entail this claim (and which we know entail this claim), such as that one played soccer at the park yesterday. Accordingly, if this hinge commitment were unknowable, then even simple closure could be marshalled to bring one's knowledge of this everyday proposition into question (since if one knew it, then one ought to be in a position to know the hinge commitment too). If hinge commitments can amount to knowledge via their entitlement status, however, then this particular sceptical line of attack is neutralised.

Of course, since simple closure has independent problems, and since as we've noted it is in any case more plausible to conceive of the radical sceptic as making use of competent deduction closure, then this point of Wright's is somewhat moot. Interestingly, the closure-style principle that Wright thinks should be rejected is effectively competent deduction closure. Wright argues that what we should conclude from our rational obligation to embrace hinge commitments is that the rational support that our beliefs enjoy does not 'transmit' across known entailments. In the case just offered, for example, although knowledge transfers across the known entailment, the rational support that one has for the everyday claim (that one played soccer at the park yesterday) doesn't transfer to being rational support for the entailed claim (that the universe didn't just come into existence moments ago) for the simple reason that the entailed claim, *qua* hinge commitment, cannot enjoy rational support.

Although there are some technical differences between the kind of 'transmission' principle that Wright is envisaging here and competent deduction closure, we can set them to one side for our purposes.[63] The key point is that since competent deduction closure demands that one's belief in the entailed proposition be based on the competent deduction from one's prior knowledge, then it

---

[63] For a useful discussion of these differences, see Wright (2022).

ought to follow from such a principle that the knowledge that results from this deduction is rationally grounded. Accordingly, where the entailed proposition is a hinge commitment that cannot be rationally grounded, then competent deduction closure is in trouble. Wright's strategy is thus to meet this issue head-on by rejecting this version of the closure principle by appealing to the essential groundlessness of our hinge commitments. Given the plausibility of competent deduction closure, this commit's Wright's approach to a significant degree of revisionism.

One puzzling aspect of Wright's position is why one would go to the trouble of retaining simple closure if one is willing to reject competent deduction closure, particularly since (as we've noted), simple closure has independent problems. Normally when philosophers respond to the radical sceptical paradox by denying the closure principle, it is because they believe that the relevant entailed anti-sceptical propositions are not known.[64] In contrast, Wright wants to maintain that they are known, albeit not in a fashion that would enable them to satisfy competent deduction closure.

Even setting this point aside, there is a question mark over whether Wright can establish that our hinge commitments are known in the manner that he sets out. One issue here is that it is hard to understand what it would be for a belief to genuinely count as knowledge if one has no rational basis for the truth of what is believed. This is why it is more natural to treat Wittgenstein as maintaining that they are not known at all. (Indeed, that they are not just unknown but also, *qua* hinge commitments, not the kind of thing that is in the market for knowledge in the first place. We will return to this point below.)

A related issue in this regard is that knowledge entails belief and yet it is not clear that the propositional attitude that we have towards our hinge commitments on Wright's view could be one of belief. This is because belief, at least in the sense relevant to knowledge (we will come back to this point), seems to be a propositional attitude that bears certain basic conceptual connections to reasons and truth. In particular, if one recognises that one has no rational basis for regarding *p* as true, then whatever one's propositional attitude towards *p*, it cannot be one of belief in this sense. Wright (e.g., 2004*b*, §2) is fully aware of this issue, as he argues that our hinge commitments are a kind of trusting rather than a form of believing. In order to continue to maintain the thought that hinge commitments are known, such that simple closure is respected, it is thus

---

[64] This was, famously, the sort of line spearheaded by Dretske (e.g., 1970) and Nozick (1981, part 3), though note that at this point in the debate about radical scepticism it was thought that the sceptical puzzle turned on simple closure rather than competent deduction closure (indeed, in Dretske's case, the idea was that it turns merely on the claim that knowledge is closed under entailments, regardless of whether the entailments are known).

necessary for Wright to weaken the connection between knowledge and belief. What's required by knowledge, it seems, is just an outright commitment to the truth of the target proposition, and not necessarily a belief in this proposition.

I think the bigger problem facing Wright's proposal is how it makes important concessions to the radical sceptic, of a kind that I would argue are contrary to what Wittgenstein was envisaging in *On Certainty*. Relatedly, I think Wright completely mischaracterises the propositional attitude involved in our hinge commitments, in that they are not assumptions or presuppositions that one is obliged to trust.

That Wright's proposal makes important concessions to radical sceptic is already apparent in the 'Serenity Prayer' quotation offered earlier. Consider also this passage:

> [*The Wittgensteinian line* . . .] concedes that the best sceptical arguments have something to teach us – that the limits of justification they bring out are genuine and essential – but then replies that, just for that reason, cognitive achievement must be reckoned to take place *within such limits*. The attempt to surpass them would result not in an increase in rigour or solidity but merely in cognitive paralysis. (Wright 2004b, 191)

Notice that by saying that radical sceptical arguments teach us something, it follows that they can't simply rest on a mistake, as in that case we could reject them wholesale. Indeed, Wright is elsewhere quite explicit that aiming to respond to the sceptical argument by showing that it rests on a mistake is a hopeless endeavour:

> But there is no disguising the fact that the exercise comes as one of damage limitation. That will disappoint those who hanker after a demonstration that there was all along, actually, no real damage to limit – that the sceptical arguments involve *mistakes*. Good luck to all philosophers who quest for such a demonstration. (Wright 2004b, 206–7)

What is surprising about this line is that it does seem very clear that Wittgenstein is offering the notion of a hinge commitment precisely as a way of showing that radical scepticism rests on a mistake. As we noted earlier, the mistake is to suppose that the very idea of universal rational evaluations is not only coherent but also grounded in our ordinary epistemic practices. In contrast, Wittgenstein is trying to get us to see that there is nothing in our ordinary epistemic practices that could license such a conception of the structure of rational evaluation. This conception of the structure of rational evaluation turns out to be not only fundamentally incoherent but also such that it is entirely alien to our ordinary epistemic practices (i.e., it is not merely a 'purified' version of them). This is the sense in which Wittgenstein is offering a powerful diagnosis of the putative radical sceptical paradox, one that shows that it is not a genuine paradox at all. If this is correct, however, then Wright is mistaken in thinking that Wittgenstein is exposing some deep sceptical truth by advancing his notion of hinge commitments, and Wright has accordingly blunted the anti-sceptical import of this notion by construing it along these lines.

I think this point is also evident in how Wright conceives of the propositional attitude involved in our hinge commitments as a trusting, with the hinges themselves functioning as assumptions or presuppositions. This is not how Wittgenstein describes them. Indeed, he explicitly contrasts our hinge commitments with assumptions (e.g., OC §343). There is a good reason for this, as Wittgenstein regards our hinge commitments as brute certainties, as we have noted earlier. Conviction of this kind is very different to trust, however, and it is certainly not the kind of propositional attitude we have to our groundless presuppositions. For example, trusting that p is compatible with agnosticism about the truth of p. Indeed, in a case where one is actively trusting a groundless presupposition, the appropriate rational stance to take towards the truth of p is precisely one of agnosticism (if not plain doubt). But Wittgenstein clearly regards our brute certainty that p as precluding any degree of hesitancy of this kind. As our actions reveal, we are fully, viscerally, committed to the truth of our hinges. Wright's conception of our hinge commitments is thus very different to that put forward by Wittgenstein.[65]

2.5 Coliva on Extended Rationality

In a series of important works, Annalisa Coliva (e.g., 2010a, 2015, 2022) has advanced a distinctive account of our hinge commitments, one that shares some core features with Wright's proposal but which also departs from it in important ways. Like Wright, Coliva's main conception of hinge commitments is as presuppositions that are essential for our cognitive lives. Unlike Wright, however, Coliva is explicit that she is offering a more restrictive account of hinge commitments than that offered by Wittgenstein himself (and hence this is a proposal that, like Williams's earlier, is merely inspired by *On Certainty* rather than being a straightforward interpretation of it).[66] For example, on Coliva's view many of the paradigmatic instances of hinge commitments that Wittgenstein discusses, such as that (in normal circumstances) one has hands,

---

[65] I expand on this point about the difference between our hinge conviction and the propositional attitude of trusting in Prichard (2023a), where I also offer a more detailed critique of Wright's position.
[66] See, especially, Coliva's contribution to Coliva, Moyal-Sharrock & Pritchard (*forthcoming*).

are not genuine hinge commitments.[67] Her examples of hinge commitments are instead the kind of necessary presuppositions of cognitive project that Wright outlines, such as that there is an external world.

One key area where Coliva departs from Wright's account is that she grants that the hinge commitments, so construed, do not amount to knowledge. Relatedly, she doesn't just reject competent deduction closure but also rejects simple closure too.[68] Accordingly, Coliva has no need of Wright's notion of entitlement (which was proposed as a way of explaining how our hinge commitments can amount to knowledge). Coliva's proposal is instead that we should adopt a different conception of epistemic rationality – what she refers to as an *extended rationality* – that is concerned not only with rational support but also with those presuppositions that are necessary for our cognitive projects.

Coliva calls such an account of hinge commitments *constitutivist*, in that the idea is that hinge commitments are constitutive of epistemic rationality even while being essentially groundless. In a Wittgensteinian spirit, they are propositions that function like epistemic norms which enable us to be epistemically rational. As such, she claims that it would be a mistake to exclude them from epistemic rationality on the grounds that they lack rational support. As she puts it, to exclude them would be akin to excluding the rules of a game from being part of the game on the grounds that they are not moves within the game.[69] In this way we are in a position to argue, in response to the radical sceptic, that our hinge presuppositions are epistemically rational even though rationally groundless. Coliva's idea is thus that the radical sceptic has been too quick to conclude from the groundlessness of our hinge commitments that they are not epistemically rational.

Many of the issues raised for Wright's proposal will transfer to Coliva's. Since Coliva, like Wright, rejects competent deduction closure, she is also committed to a high level of revisionism. There is also the question of whether she has captured the notion of a hinge commitment correctly, even granted her restricted emphasis in this regard. We've already noted that it seems Wittgenstein's view was that a statement like 'There is an external world' is in fact meaningless, in which case it cannot function as a contentful hinge commitment. More generally, it is significant that Wittgenstein's focus when it comes to hinge commitments is not on general presumptions of inquiry but

---

[67] A distinction that is often made in the literature is between local, or *de facto*, hinge commitments and universal, or *de jure*, hinge commitments, with many of Wittgenstein's favoured examples of hinge commitments (such as the hands example) falling on the former side of the distinction. See, for example, Moyal-Sharrock (2005, chs. 5 & 7). In terms of this distinction, Coliva is arguing that the only genuine hinges are de jure hinge commitments.

[68] See especially Coliva (2014).   [69] See Coliva, Moyal-Sharrock & Pritchard (*forthcoming*).

rather on mundane everyday claims. Relatedly, the relevant propositional attitude doesn't seem to be a presuppositional one at all, but rather a brute, visceral outright conviction. We will return to these points below.

2.6 Greco on Common Knowledge

John Greco (2016) has recently put forward an intriguing proposal regarding how to understand the notion of a hinge commitment. He argues that we should regard them as knowledge but of a particular kind, what he refers to as 'common knowledge'. This is a kind of background, tacit knowledge that is generally accepted within one's epistemic community. It also has a further, crucial, feature on Greco's account, which is that it is form of knowledge that one gets for 'free', without having to do any cognitive work, which makes is completely unlike other forms of knowledge. The analogy that Greco has in mind here is that of common property. Here is Greco:

> In addition to the categories of generated knowledge and transmitted knowledge, each governed by the norms appropriate to their distinctive function, we should allow that there is a third such category – that of *common knowledge*. Common knowledge would be analogous to common or public property – roughly speaking, everyone gets to use it for free. On this extended model, there is knowledge that you produce for yourself, knowledge that someone gives you, and common knowledge that is available for everyone. (Greco 2016, 320)

Greco argues that thinking of our hinge commitments in terms of common knowledge can explain some of their most distinctive properties. For example, it seems to make no sense to claim to know one's hinge commitments in ordinary contexts. If they are the kind of thing which everyone knows, then of course no practical purpose is served by stating them. Or consider that one lacks a rational basis for believing one's hinge commitments. On Greco's proposal this merely reflects the fact that these are common knowledge and thus a kind of knowledge that one has without grounds, simply by being part of the relevant epistemic community. Similarly, that we aren't explicitly taught our hinge commitments, but rather 'swallow them down' in what we are explicitly taught (OC §143), can be accounted for by how common knowledge is tacitly presupposed in a practice rather than made explicit.

Greco further motivates his account by appealing to his wider epistemological views about what he calls the 'information economy'.[70] This is the set of norms that 'govern the acquisition and distribution of actionable information (information that can be used in action and practical reasoning) within

---

[70] See Greco (2020).

a community of information sharers' (Greco 2016, 318). Greco claims that there are two core activities involved in the information economy. On the one hand, there will be activities concerned with the acquisition and gathering of knowledge – here the relevant epistemic norms will serve, as Greco puts it, a 'gate-keeping' function to ensure that only information that is of epistemically good quality enters the system. On the other hand, there will be activities associated with the distribution of knowledge, such as via testimonial routes like education, news sources and so on. As Greco points out, since the gate-keeping function is served by the epistemic norms covering the acquisition and gathering of knowledge, so the epistemic norms associated with the distribution of knowledge can be relatively permissive, as their role is not to keep out sub-standard information but rather to ensure the flow of *bona fide* knowledge within the system. Greco's idea is that common knowledge can fit into this system of norms by being a kind of knowledge where there is no need for any gate-keeping requirement and hence which is freely available to all:

> The idea is that such knowledge can be freed up for common use without further concern for quality control. It is so well known, and so widely known, that we are happy to grant it to everyone. (Greco 2016, 321)

Hinge commitments are thus a kind of knowledge on Greco's view, albeit knowledge of a special kind that one acquires without needing to expend any cognitive effort.

While this is an intriguing suggestion, it doesn't really stand up to closer scrutiny. For one thing, it is hard to see how Greco's appeal to an information economy is meant to be compatible with common knowledge that one can acquire without meeting any epistemic standard. The very notion of an information economy as Greco presents it is wedded to the idea that there can be a variable gate-keeping role, but that entails that there is always *some* degree of epistemic hurdle required for knowledge – knowledge is never 'free'. But the more important issue for our purposes is that this proposal is not a good way of thinking about hinge commitments. In order to bring out why this is so, it will be useful to first discuss an important exegetical issue that bears on this discussion.

Greco makes a mistake in reading in *On Certainty* that I think afflicts many readers of this work, which is to suppose that every certainty that Wittgenstein discusses is a hinge commitment. We've already noted one pitfall with this approach, which is that the Moorean certainty that there is an external world is treated by Wittgenstein as simply nonsense, in which case it cannot be a hinge commitment at all. But there is a further reason why Greco's approach is problematic in this respect. This is that a close reading of *On Certainty* reveals that Wittgenstein is contrasting two kinds of everyday certainty, one that he treats as knowledge (roughly, 'common knowledge', though it's not quite as Greco describes it) and another that he treats as a hinge certainty and which isn't regarded as knowledge. Admittedly, with *On Certainty* being composed of notebooks that Wittgenstein never got the chance to edit, the distinction is not always very clear, but if one reads the notebooks as a whole the contrast is returned to again and again, and becomes increasingly explicit as one moves through the notebooks (as if this is a distinction that Wittgenstein is developing via his jottings).

I noted earlier that what is central to Wittgenstein's conception of a hinge commitment to a specific proposition is the relation that it bears to the über hinge commitment, which is the overarching visceral certainty in one's worldview. This is why our hinge commitments are mundane commonsense nodes in our worldview, such as that one has hands, since these are precisely the kinds of claims which, if false, would call one's worldview as a whole into question. As Wittgenstein puts it, a doubt here would 'drag everything with it and plunge it into chaos' (OC §613). The thought is thus that one's visceral certainty in these everyday commonsense claims is essentially a manifestation of one's overarching über hinge certainty in one's worldview. This is why these are essentially groundless commitments, since they inherit this property from the über hinge commitment.

Many of the everyday certainties that Wittgenstein discusses in *On Certainty* are not manifestations of the über hinge commitment in this way, however. Consider, for example, a statement like 'water boils when heated', which is an example of an everyday certainty that Wittgenstein considers in a number of passages in *On Certainty* (e.g., OC §338, §555, §558, §613). While Wittgenstein notes that this is something that we all are certain of, he also treats it as an instance of knowledge. Indeed, Wittgenstein's thought seems to be that with statements like this we have captured a kind of everyday knowledge that is so widely shared that it effectively functions as part of the – usually *tacit* – *common* epistemic background of our practices. One might thus call it 'common knowledge'. Note, however, that the suggestion is not that this is knowledge that one gets for free, like the notion of common knowledge that Greco proposes. Instead, Wittgenstein is highlighting a kind of everyday knowledge that we are certain of which is evidentially grounded. As he puts it with regard to this example of water boiling when heated, experience has shown us that it is true:

> We say we know that water boils when it is put over a fire. How do we know? Experience has taught us. (OC §555)

The thought is thus not that this is a kind of common knowledge that we acquire without clearing any epistemic hurdle, but rather that it is knowledge that is easy to acquire because the grounds for this knowledge are so readily available.

The everyday certainties that amount to common knowledge in this way are very different from our hinge certainties. We've already noted that the former is evidentially supported and known, while the latter is essentially arational. But the more significant divergence is that only the latter is a manifestation of the overarching über hinge commitment. By the time we get to the fourth, and final, notebook that makes up *On Certainty*, Wittgenstein is increasingly explicit about this contrast and its implications. Consider, for example, this passage, where Wittgenstein compares the certainty of the common knowledge that water will boil when heated, as opposed to the hinge commitment that the dear friend in plain view in front of him is who he appears to be:

> If I now say 'I know that the water in the kettle in the gas-flame will not freeze but boil', I seem to be as justified in this 'I know' as I am in any. 'If I know anything I know this'. – Or do I know with still greater certainty that the person opposite me is my old friend so-and-so? ... But still there is a difference between cases. If the water over the gas freezes, of course I shall be as astonished as can be, but I shall assume some factor I don't know of, and perhaps leave the matter to physicists to judge. But what could make me doubt whether this person here is N.N., whom I have known for years? Here a doubt would seem to drag everything with it and plunge it into chaos. (OC §613)

Wittgenstein's point is that not everything that we are completely confident of is a hinge commitment. In the case of the common knowledge certainties, in particular, doubt of them wouldn't call into the question the über hinge commitment (and thereby 'drag everything into chaos') but would merely be very puzzling. This highlights that there is a very different kind of certainty in play. It is, however, the distinctive kind of certainty that is associated with the über hinge commitment that is the hinge commitment.

By uncritically listing a bunch of certainties that are discussed by Wittgenstein in *On Certainty* as hinge commitments, Greco has overlooked this important distinction. For some of the examples that he offers, it would be plausible to conceive of them as common knowledge, but that is precisely because they are not genuine hinge commitments. For other examples, where a genuine hinge commitment is in play, the idea that these commitments amount to knowledge is not a credible reading of *On Certainty*.

Understanding that Wittgenstein's discussion in *On Certainty* is in part aimed at distinguishing common knowledge certainties from hinge commitments is also relevant to Williams's treatment of this notion that we examined earlier. As we noted, Williams thinks that our hinge commitments are known, even though we lack any rational basis for them. In this regard they are very much akin to common knowledge in Greco's sense, in that they are knowledge that we get for free. Williams is led to this interpretation because of the fact that Wittgenstein describes a number of certainties in *On Certainty* as knowledge. But I think a more plausible reading of *On Certainty* would regard these remarks as being concerned not with our hinge certainties but rather with our common knowledge certainties.[71]

2.7 Pritchard on Our Visceral Hinge Commitments

The foregoing discussion will likely have given the reader a good sense of where I stand on this debate about hinge commitments. There are two elements of my reading of *On Certainty* that should be highlighted. The first is that I want to take seriously how Wittgenstein's primary concern in this regard is to capture the certainty that permeates our worldview, with our hinge commitments to specific propositions flowing from this overarching über hinge certainty. The second is to embrace what Wittgenstein says about the visceral, animal, brute nature of our hinge commitments.

By placing the über hinge certainty at the heart of the proposal, we gain a plausible story about why our hinge certainties should play a framework role in our rational practices, whereby they enable such practices without thereby subject to rational evaluations themselves. The idea that one cannot justify one's worldview as a whole, such that rational evaluations must necessarily be undertaken from within that worldview, is independently plausible, since where would one stand to undertake such a wholesale rational evaluation? That acquiring a worldview at all, such that one can even be in the space of reasons, requires this permeating certainty in the worldview is surely an innovation on Wittgenstein's part, but it is no less compelling for it. Once we see this certainty as an essential backdrop to our rational evaluations, then we can also understand how it will manifest itself in particular commonsense commitments that lie at the very heart of that worldview. That is, our hinge certainties are not theoretical claims, like the presuppositional generalities at issue in Wright and Coliva's proposals, much less are they philosophical theses (such as about an external world), but are rather, for the most part anyway, utterly mundane, everyday claims.

Moreover, such hinge certainty must, perforce, be animal, rather than rational, in nature, something that is grounded in our actions rather than our reasons. This is why our hinge commitments are very different to trustings, as they are a propositional attitude that is by its nature incompatible with any kind

---

[71] I discuss Greco's proposal in more detail in Pritchard (2022*b*). See also Coliva (2023).

of intellectual distance from the target proposition (such as agnosticism about the truth of that proposition). One shows one's complete conviction in one's hinge commitments, and thus in one's worldview, in one's actions. *Contra* Moyal-Sharrock's reading, I think we can capture this sense of the primacy of action without going so far as to regard our hinge certainty as non-propositional in nature. Nonetheless, since I emphasise the visceral, action-based, nature of our hinge commitments, of the proposals we have considered in this section mine is probably the closest in spirit to Moyal-Sharrock's reading.[72]

Taking these aspects of Wittgenstein's remarks in *On Certainty* seriously is crucial to recognising their anti-sceptical appeal. Like Williams, I regard Wittgenstein's underlying insight to be that the radical sceptical paradox is illusory. The point is not just, *à la* Strawson, that we simply cannot doubt certain empirical claims, but rather that it is in the very nature of rational evaluations that they presuppose a framework of arational certainty. It follows that the very idea that there can be fully general rational evaluations is simply incoherent. Moreover, Wittgenstein is trying to get us to see how sceptical doubts are not just unnatural but positively alien to our normal epistemic practices, such that their employment cannot be plausibly cast as mere refinements of those practices.

On my view of hinge commitments, they are essentially arational and hence unknown. I would argue, however, that it would be misleading to *simply* describe them as unknown, as if we take seriously Wittgenstein's point about the necessity of our groundless hinge commitments to our practices of rational evaluation, then it follows that they are not even in the market for knowledge. It is not as if, for example, we are *ignorant* of our hinge commitments, as would apply to a proposition that we ought to know but fail to.[73] This marks a fundamental difference between my account and that offered by, for example, someone like Wright, who treats Wittgenstein as highlighting how radical scepticism reveals a fundamental cognitive limitation on our parts. I would rather claim that it no more reveals a cognitive limitation on one's part that one cannot know

---

[72] A possible exception in this regard is Schönbaumsfeld's (2016) provocative reading of *On Certainty*. Space prevents me from undertaking a detailed discussion of this complex work, but one key element of her view that is of note for our current purposes is that while she follows the authors in this part in treating our hinge commitments as propositional in nature, she not only rejects the idea that they are knowledge but also that they are even certainties. In essence, her claim is that certainty and knowledge are categories that only have application where doubt is possible, something that is excluded by the nature of our hinge commitments. For a useful recent symposium on this work, see Moyal-Sharrock (2021), Ranalli (2021*a*) Schönbaumsfeld (2021*a*, 2021*b*) and Williams (2021*b*).

[73] Note that this observation that one is not ignorant of one's hinge commitments illustrates the more general point that there is more to ignorance than simply a lack of knowledge. See Pritchard (2021*b*, 2021*c*).

one's hinge commitments than the fact that one cannot imagine a circle-square reveals an imaginative limitation.

Nonetheless, one might wonder how, exactly, my line on hinge commitments responds to the radical sceptical paradox. Since I claim that our hinge commitments are unknown, then does that mean that I deny competent deduction closure, like Wright and Coliva? As I noted earlier, I regard taking such a route out of radical sceptical paradox to be highly revisionary, given the centrality of this principle to our ordinary epistemic practices. Relatedly, if one is truly showing that the radical sceptical paradox is illusory, then it ought to be possible to dissolve the appearance of paradox without making any major concessions, for otherwise that would be to concede that there is a genuine tension in play here (and hence would imply that the paradox is real after all).

If one takes seriously what Wittgenstein says about the nature of the propositional attitude involved in our hinge commitments, however, then there is no need to deny competent deduction closure, even though our hinge commitments are unknown. Recall that competent deduction closure is a diachronic principle concerned with the formation of belief on the basis of a competent deduction from one's knowledge. Moreover, we also noted that it was crucial that closure is formulated in this way if it is to serve its intended role in the formulation of the radical sceptical paradox, as alternative formulations are open to independent problems. I noted earlier that on my view our hinge commitments to specific propositions are usually utterly mundane everyday propositions, such as concerning one's hands or what one's name is. There is, however, a class of non-everyday propositions that are also hinge commitments on this view, and that is the denials of radical sceptical hypotheses. After all, such hypotheses are designed to call one's beliefs into question en masse, and hence are a direct challenge to one's über hinge commitment. Accordingly, one's groundless über hinge certainty transfers to a groundless hinge certainty in the denials of these hypotheses. The problem posed by competent deduction closure is that it seems we ought to be able to come to know the denials of these hypotheses by undertaking competent deductions from the myriad quotidian propositions that we know. Conversely, if we deny that our hinge commitments are known, then doesn't that entail that competent deduction closure has to go?

In order for there to be this tension between our lack of knowledge of the denials of radical sceptical hypotheses and competent deduction closure, however, it is important that one's hinge commitments can be a belief that one can acquire via a paradigmatically rational process like competent deduction. On both counts, however, Wittgenstein shows us that our hinge commitments are just not the sort of propositional attitude that could play this role. That one can't acquire one's hinge commitments via rational processes ought to be clear from how we have characterised them. But what about the idea that our hinge commitments cannot be beliefs?

The folk notion of belief is highly permissive in that it encompasses a range of propositional attitudes, including such diverse propositional attitudes as those involved in religious faith, scientific acceptance, educated guesses and so on.[74] Indeed, it is sufficient to count as believing that *p* in the folk sense that one sincerely endorses *p*. In the folk sense of belief, hinge commitments are beliefs. But it is not the folk sense of belief that is at issue in competent deduction closure, as this needs to be belief in the sense of that propositional attitude that is a constituent part of knowledge, given that we are meant to come to know what we come to believe via the target competent deduction. Elsewhere I have called this propositional attitude *K-apt belief*.[75] We noted earlier that Wright was wary about thinking of our hinge commitments as beliefs, but I think that this concern, properly understood, relates to thinking of them specifically as K-apt beliefs, which is the relevant propositional attitude in our discussion of radical scepticism. K-apt beliefs bear certain basic conceptual connections to reasons and truth. In particular, we noted earlier that one feature of K-apt belief is that one cannot K-apt believe that *p* while being aware that one has no rational basis for the truth of *p*. Crucially, however, our hinge commitments fail such a condition, as becoming aware of the groundlessness of our hinge commitments doesn't undermine our certainty in them at all, as we continue to act with complete conviction just as before.[76]

The upshot is that while our hinge commitments might be beliefs in the folk sense, they are not K-apt beliefs. If that's right, then the putative radical sceptical paradox never materialises as competent deduction closure is simply inapplicable to our hinge commitments. In particular, the fact that one cannot know one's hinge commitments cannot pose a problem for competent deduction closure given that it is impossible to acquire a K-apt belief in them via the target deduction. This means that the radical sceptical paradox is shown to be illusory

---

[74] It is thus a 'suitcase' term, to borrow Minsky's (2007) terminology. Indeed, as a number of commentators have noted, the folk notion of belief is often used to describe the propositional attitudes involves in delusions too, even when the delusions are quite profound. See Pritchard (2024a, 2024c) for discussion of this point. For a helpful survey of a range of different ways in which the folk notion of belief is employed, see Stevenson (2002).

[75] For further discussion of this notion, see Pritchard (2015b, part 2, 2018a, 2024c).

[76] This is not to suggest that becoming aware of the groundlessness of our hinge commitments doesn't generate any kind of intellectual anxiety, only that it is not an anxiety that could manifests itself in an actual doubt. Drawing on the work of Cavell (especially 1979), who unfortunately never seriously engaged with *On Certainty*, I have argued that recognizing one's hinge commitments as hinge commitments can lead to a phenomenon that I call *epistemic vertigo*. See Pritchard (2015a, part 4, 2019b, 2020). For the relevance of Cavell's work on the later Wittgenstein (albeit not with regard to *On Certainty*) in this regard, see Pritchard (2021a, 2024b).

in that the three elements that make up this paradox – our widespread knowledge, our inability to know the denials of radical sceptical hypotheses and competent deduction closure – turn out to be compatible with one another. Taking Wittgenstein's remarks about the visceral nature of our hinge commitments seriously is thus important to unpacking the diagnostic aspect of his anti-scepticism and thereby showing that the putative radical sceptical paradox is in fact illusory. Radical scepticism is shown to be the product of faulty philosophical theory rather than arising out of fundamental tensions within our own ordinary epistemic practices.[77]

2.8 Concluding Remarks: New Directions

I have focussed on different conceptions of hinge commitments in contemporary epistemology and their supposed relevance to the problem of radical scepticism. I want to close by considering some of the ways in which the contemporary epistemological debate about hinge commitments has begun to spread to other topics. I will mention two in particular: epistemic relativism and religious hinges.

There is an obvious route from discussions of hinge commitments to the topic of epistemic relativism. If our hinge commitments provide the framework for our rational evaluations, and if we can have variable hinge commitments, then the concern naturally arises that there might different epistemic frameworks. On the positive side, such a conclusion looks like it might allow us to use hinge commitments to make sense of what are known as *deep disagreements* – that is, disagreements that seem to be particularly intractable in that they concern diverging fundamental commitments that each party holds with great enthusiasm. Could it be that such deep disagreements are to be understood as clashes of hinge commitments by subjects employing distinct epistemic frameworks (on account of the fact that they have distinct hinge commitments)?

---

[77] I develop my reading of *On Certainty* in a number of places, but see especially Pritchard (2015a, *passim*). See also Pritchard (2012b, 2018b). One topic regarding *On Certainty* and contemporary responses to radical scepticism that I didn't have space to cover here is the question of whether Wittgenstein is answering not only closure-based radical scepticism but also a different kind of radical sceptical argument that turns on an epistemic principle known as the *underdetermination principle* (roughly, that one's rational support in paradigm cases is no better than it would be in corresponding cases where one is the victim of a radical sceptical hypothesis). See Pritchard (2015a, *passim*) for a detailed discussion of this distinction and an argument to the effect that Wittgenstein's hinge commitment line only applies to closure-based scepticism. Williams (1991) effectively treats these two forms of radical scepticism as co-extensive, and applies his hinge commitment line to both – see Pritchard (2018d) for a critical discussion. Interestingly, Schönbaumsfeld (2016) argues that the underdetermination-based sceptical argument is fundamental in this regard and that Wittgenstein is primarily answering this challenge. See also Schönbaumsfeld (2019).

On the negative side, there is the concern that taking hinge commitments seriously and allowing for there to be significant divergences in our hinge commitments can lead to not just distinct epistemic systems but epistemically incommensurate epistemic systems. That is, if the divergence in hinge commitments is significant enough, then perhaps there can be deep hinge disagreements that are even in principle unresolvable by rational means due to the lack of sufficient overlap in the competing epistemic systems. Accordingly, one issue that is very important in this regard is understanding just how extensive divergences of hinge commitments can be, something that obviously depends on how one understands this notion.[78]

The second topic is related to the first. Following Wittgenstein's lead, the usual examples of hinge commitments, as we have seen, tend to be mostly ordinary empirical commitments. It is natural to wonder, however, whether this notion could be extended to a broader range of propositions that capture what we might term our axiological commitments. Could there, for example, be moral, political, or religious hinge commitments? The specific question of religious hinge commitments has generated the most discussion in this respect (though there is now a nascent literature on moral hinge commitments).[79] One can see the attraction, given that fundamental religious commitments seem to have much in common with hinge commitments, such as their resistance to evidence, their high levels of conviction, the way that they are absorbed as part of being taught a worldview and so on. Allowing that there can be religious hinge commitments (or, for that matter, axiological hinge commitments more generally) relates to the topic of epistemic relativism in that it can potentially exacerbate the worry we noted earlier about epistemic incommensurability. This is because of the wide divergence found in fundamental religious commitments and how this entails quite radical differences in one's worldview.

I have described the epistemology of religious belief that turns on religious hinge commitments as *quasi-fideism*.[80] The view is fideistic to the extent that it treats fundamental religious commitments as arational. It also departs from traditional forms of fideism, however, in that it doesn't treat religious belief as being in general a matter of faith nor does it treat the epistemology of religious

---

[78] For some of the recent literature devoted to this topic, see Coliva (2010b, 2019), Pritchard (2010a, 2018e, 2023b), Kusch (2016), Carter (2017), Moyal-Sharrock (2017), Coliva & Palmira (2020), Ranalli (2020), and Siegel (2021).

[79] See, for example, Johnson (2019) and Ranalli (2021b).

[80] I discuss quasi-fideism and its implications in Pritchard (2011b, 2015b, 2017a, 2018c, 2021d, 2022a, 2022d, 2024a, *forthcominga*; *forthcomingc*). For some recent critical discussions of the proposal, see di Ceglie (2017), Ljiljanaa & Slavišab (2017), Bennett-Hunter (2019), de Ridder (2019), Gascoigne (2019, *passim*), Gomez-Alonso (2021), Smith (2021), Boncompagni (2022), Vinten (2022), Aquino & Gage (2023), Coliva (2024) and Williams (*forthcoming*).

belief differently from the epistemology of non-religious belief. Quasi-fideism is thus a very different position to the usual fideism that is often attributed (with good cause) to the later Wittgenstein.[81] The proposal is also significant in that it sets out a position in the epistemology of religion literature that has hitherto been unexplored.[82]

---

[81] This is usually attributed on the basis of the remarks in Wittgenstein (1966). For some discussions of Wittgensteinian fideism, see Nielsen (1967) and Philips (1976). See also Bell (1995).

[82] DMS: Thanks to Brendan Larvor, Duncan Pritchard. Work on this monograph was completed thanks to a research leave granted by the University of Hertfordshire. DHP: Thanks to Annalisa Coliva, Danièle Moyal-Sharrock, and Genia Schönbaumsfeld. Work on this monograph was completed while a Senior Research Associate of the *African Centre for Epistemology and Philosophy of Science* at the University of Johannesburg. We are both grateful to David Stern and two anonymous reviewers for their comments on an earlier version of this manuscript.

Abbreviations of Wittgenstein's Works

AWL	*Wittgenstein's Lectures: Cambridge, 1932–1935*, from the notes of A. Ambrose & M. MacDonald, ed. A. Ambrose (Oxford: Blackwell, 1979).
BT	*The Big Typescript: TS 213*, ed. & trans. by C. Grant Luckhardt & Maximilian A. E. Aue (Oxford: Blackwell, 2005).
CE	'Cause and Effect: Intuitive Awareness', in PO, 371–426.
LE	'A Lecture on Ethics', in *Philosophical Occasions: 1912–1951*, eds. J. C. Klagge & A. Nordman, 37–44 (Indianapolis: Hackett, 1993).
LPE	'Notes for Lectures on 'Private Experience' and 'Sense Data'', in PO, 202–367.
LW I	*Last Writings on the Philosophy of Psychology* [1948–1949], vol I, eds. G. H. von Wright & H. Nyman, trans. C. G. Luckhardt & M. A. E. Aue (Oxford: Blackwell, 1982).
LW II	*Last Writings on the Philosophy of Psychology* [1949–1951], vol II, eds. G. H. von Wright & H. Nyman, trans. C. G. Luckhardt & M. A. E. Aue (Oxford: Blackwell,1992).
OC	*On Certainty*, eds. G. E. M. Anscombe & G. H. von Wright, trans. D. Paul & G. E. M. Anscombe, amended 1st ed. (Oxford: Blackwell, 1997).
PG	*Philosophical Grammar*, ed. R. Rhees, trans. A. Kenny (Oxford: Blackwell, 1974).
PI	*Philosophical Investigations*, trans. G. E. M. Anscombe, 2nd ed. (Oxford: Blackwell, 1997).
PO	*Philosophical Occasions: 1912–1951*, eds. J. C. Klagge & A. Nordman (Indianapolis: Hackett, 1993).
PR	*Philosophical Remarks*, ed. R. Rhees, trans. R. Hargreaves & R. White (Oxford: Blackwell, 1975).
RFM	*Remarks on the Foundations of Mathematics*. [1937–1944] Third Edition. Edited by G.H. von Wright, R. Rhees, G. E. M. Anscombe. Translated by G. E. M. Anscombe (Oxford: Basil Blackwell, 1978).
RPP I	*Remarks on the Philosophy of Psychology* [1945–1947], vol I, eds. G. E. M. Anscombe & G.H. von Wright, trans. G. E. M. Anscombe (Oxford: Blackwell, 1980).
RPP II	*Remarks on the Philosophy of Psychology* [1948], vol II, eds. G. H. von Wright & H. Nyman, trans. C. G. Luckhardt & M. A. E. Aue (Oxford: Blackwell, 1980).

TLP　　*Tractatus Logico-Philosophicus*, trans. D. F. Pears & B. F. McGuinness (London: Routledge & Kegan Paul, 1961).

WVC　　*Ludwig Wittgenstein and the Vienna Circle*, shorthand notes recorded by F. Waismann, ed. B. F. McGuinness (Oxford: Blackwell, 1979).

References

Aquino, F. D., & Gage, L. P. (2023). 'Newman and Quasi-Fideism: A Reply to Duncan Pritchard', *Heythrop Journal* 64, 695–706. https://doi.org/10.1111/heyj.14244.

Bazin J. (2002). 'Si un lion . . . ', *Philosophia Scientiæ*, 6, 127–46.

Bell, R. H. (1995). 'Religion and Wittgenstein's Legacy: Beyond Fideism and Language Games', in *Philosophy and the Grammar of Religious Belief* (eds.) T. Tessin & M. von der Ruhr, 215–48, London: Palgrave Macmillan.

Bennett-Hunter, G. (2019). 'Wittgensteinian Quasi-Fideism and Interreligious Communication', in *Interpreting Interreligious Relations with Wittgenstein: Philosophy, Theology and Religious Studies* (eds.) G. Andrejč & D. H. Weiss, 157–73, Leiden: Brill.

Boncompagni, A. (2022). 'Religious Hinges: Some Historical Precursors', *Topoi* 41, 955–65.

Burge, T. (1993). 'Content Preservation', *Philosophical Review* 102, 457–88.

(2003). 'Perceptual Entitlement', *Philosophy and Phenomenological Research* 67, 503–48.

Callanan, J. J. (2011). 'Making Sense of Doubt: Strawson's Anti-Scepticism', *Theoria* 77, 261–78.

Carter, J. A. (2017). 'Epistemic Pluralism, Epistemic Relativism and "Hinge" Epistemology', in *Epistemic Pluralism* (eds.) A. Coliva & N. J. L. L. Pedersen, 229–52, London: Palgrave.

Cassam, Q. (2007). *The Possibility of Knowledge*, Oxford: Oxford University Press.

Cavell, S. (1979). *The Claim of Reason: Wittgenstein, Skepticism, Morality, and Tragedy*, Cambridge, MA: Harvard University Press.

Cohen, S. (1999). 'Contextualism, Skepticism, and the Structure of Reasons', *Philosophical Perspectives* 13, 57–89.

Coliva, A. (2010a). *Moore and Wittgenstein: Scepticism, Certainty and Common Sense*, London: Palgrave Macmillan.

(2010b). 'Was Wittgenstein an Epistemic Relativist?', *Philosophical Investigations* 33, 1–23.

(2013). 'Hinges and Certainty. A Précis of Moore and Wittgenstein: Scepticism, Certainty and Common Sense', *Philosophia* 41, 1–12.

(2014). 'Moderatism, Transmission Failures, Closure, and Humean Scepticism', *Scepticism and Perceptual Justification* (eds.) D. Dodd & E. Zardini, 248–72, Oxford: Oxford University Press.

(2015). *Extended Rationality: A Hinge Epistemology*, London: Palgrave Macmillan.

(2016) 'Which Hinge Epistemology?' *International Journal for the Study of Skepticism*, 6 (2–3), 79–96.

(2019). 'Hinge Epistemology and Relativism', in *Routledge Handbook of Philosophy of Relativism* (ed.) M. Kusch, 320–28, London: Routledge.

(2022). *Wittgenstein Rehinged*, London: Anthem.

(2023). 'Hinges in the Knowledge Economy: On Greco's Common and Procedural Knowledge', *Synthese* 201, 1–18.

(2024). 'Religious Hinges?', *manuscript*.

Coliva, A., & Moyal-Sharrock, D. (eds.). (2017). *Hinge Epistemology*, Leiden: Brill.

Coliva, A., Moyal-Sharrock, D. & Pritchard, D. H. (*Forthcoming*). 'Moyal-Sharrock's, Pritchard's and Coliva's Wittgenstein: The Hinge Epistemology Program', in *Wittgenstein and Other Philosophers: His Influence on Historical and Contemporary Analytic Philosophers* (Vol. I) (eds.) A. Hossein Khani & G. Kemp, London: Routledge.

Coliva, A., & Palmira, M. (2020). 'Hinge Disagreement', *Social Epistemology and Epistemic Relativism* (ed.) M. Kusch, 11–29, London: Routledge.

Coliva, A., & Pritchard, D. H. (2022). *Scepticism*, London: Routledge.

Crary, A., & Read, R. (eds.). (2000). *The New Wittgenstein*, London: Routledge.

DeRose, K. (1995). 'Solving the Skeptical Problem', *Philosophical Review* 104, 1–52.

di Ceglie, R. (2017). 'Faith and Reason: A Response to Duncan Pritchard,' *Philosophy* 92, 231–47.

de Ridder, J. (2019). 'Against Quasi-Fideism', *Faith and Philosophy* 36, 223–43.

Dretske, F. (1970). 'Epistemic Operators', *Journal of Philosophy* 67, 1007–23.

Egan, D. (2021). 'Rule Following, Anxiety, and Authenticity', *Mind* 130, 567–93.

Gascoigne, N. (2019). *Rorty, Liberal Democracy, and Religious Certainty*, London: Bloomsbury.

Gettier, E. (1963). 'Is Justified True Belief Knowledge?', *Analysis* 23, 121–23.

Glock, H.-J. (2024) 'Philosophy Rehinged?' in his *Normativity, Meaning and Philosophy: Essays on Wittgenstein*, 63–88, London: Anthem.

Gomez-Alonso, M. (2021). 'Wittgenstein, Religious Belief, and Hinge Epistemology', *Skepsis* 12, 18–34.

References

Greco, J. (2016). 'Common Knowledge', *International Journal for the Study of Skepticism* 6, 309–25.

(2020). *The Transmission of Knowledge*, Cambridge: Cambridge University Press.

Greenough, P., & Pritchard, D. H. (eds.). (2009). *Williamson on Knowledge*, Oxford: Oxford University Press.

Hacker, P. M. S. (2001). 'When the Whistling Had to Stop', in his *Wittgenstein: Connections and Controversies*, 141–69, Oxford: Oxford University Press.

Hankinson, R. J. (1998). 'Pyrrhonism', *Routledge Encyclopedia of Philosophy*, www.rep.routledge.com/articles/thematic/pyrrhonism/v-1.

Harrison, B. (2013). 'The Epistemology of Know-How', PhD thesis, University of Hertfordshire.

Hawthorne, J. (2005). 'The Case for Closure', in *Contemporary Debates in Epistemology* (eds.) E. Sosa & M. Steup, 26–43, Oxford: Blackwell.

Hutto, D. (2014). 'Contentless Perceiving: The very idea', in *Wittgenstein and Perception* (eds.) M. Campbell & M. O'Sullivan, 63–83, London: Routledge.

Johnson, D. (2019). 'Hinge Epistemology, Radical Skepticism, and Domain Specific Skepticism', *International Journal for the Study of Skepticism* 9, 116–33.

Kusch, M. (2016). 'Wittgenstein's *On Certainty* and Relativism', in *Analytic and Continental Philosophy: Methods and Perspectives* (eds.) S. Rinofner-Kreidl & H. A. Wiltsche, 29–46, Berlin: Walter de Gruyter, 29–46.

Lagerspetz, O. (2021). 'The Linguistic Idealism Question: Wittgenstein's Method and His Rejection of Realism', *Wittgenstein-Studien* 12, 37–60.

Lewis, D. (1996). 'Elusive Knowledge', *Australasian Journal of Philosophy* 74, 549–67.

Ljiljanaa, R., & Slavišab, K. (2017). 'Religious Hinge Commitments: Developing Wittgensteinian Quasi-Fideism', *Belgrade Philosophical Annual* 30, 235–56.

Malcolm, N. (1952). 'Knowledge & Belief', *Mind* 61, 178–89.

(1982). 'Wittgenstein: The Relation of Language to Instinctive Behaviour', in *Wittgenstein Themes: Essays 1978–1989*, (ed.) G. H. von Wright, 66–86, London: Cornell University Press.

(1995) 'Wittgenstein and Idealism', in *Wittgensteinian Themes: Essays 1978–1989* (ed.) G. H. von Wright, 87–109, London: Cornell University Press.

References

  (2018). 'A Memoir', in *Portraits of Wittgenstein: Abridged Edition* (eds.) F. A. Flowers III & I. Ground, 619–72, London: Bloomsbury Academic.
Malmgrem, H. (1983). *Immediate Knowledge: A Study in G. E. Moore's Epistemology*, Sweden: Doxa.
McGinn, M. (1989). *Sense and Certainty: A Dissolution of Scepticism*, Oxford: Blackwell.
  (2010). 'Ludwig Wittgenstein', in *Routledge Companion to Epistemology* (eds.) S. Bernecker & D. H. Pritchard, 763–73, London: Routledge.
Minsky, M. (2007). *The Emotion Machine: Commonsense Thinking, Artificial Intelligence, and the Future of the Human Mind*, New York: Simon & Schuster.
Moore, G. E. (1925). 'A Defence of Common Sense', in *Philosophical Papers*, 32–59, London: George Unwin, 1959.
Moore, G. E. (1939). 'Proof of an External World', in his *Philosophical Papers*, 127–50, London: George Unwin.
  (1957). *Some Main Problems of Philosophy*, Leicester: Blackfriars Press.
Morawetz, T. (1979). *Wittgenstein and Knowledge: The Importance of 'On Certainty*, Cambridge, MA: Harvester Press.
Moyal-Sharrock, D. (2002). 'The Third Wittgenstein and the Category Mistake of Philosophical Scepticism', in *Wittgenstein and the Future of Philosophy: A Reassessment after 50 Years* (eds.) R. Haller & K. Puhl, 293–305, Vienna: öbv & hpt.
  (2003). 'Logic in Action: Wittgenstein's Logical Pragmatism and the Impotence of Scepticism', *Philosophical Investigations* 26, 125–48.
  (2004). *The Third Wittgenstein: The post-Investigations works*, London: Routledge.
  (2005). *Understanding Wittgenstein's on Certainty*, London: Palgrave Macmillan.
  (2007*a*). 'The Good Sense of Nonsense: A Reading of Wittgenstein's *Tractatus* as Nonself-Repudiating', *Philosophy* 82, 147–77.
  (2007*b*). 'Wittgenstein on Psychological Certainty', in *Perspicuous Presentations: Essays on Wittgenstein's Philosophy of Psychology* (ed.) D. Moyal-Sharrock, 211–35, London: Palgrave Macmillan.
  (2016). 'The Animal in Epistemology: Wittgenstein's Enactivist Solution to the Problem of Regress', *Hinge Epistemology* (eds.) A. Coliva & D. Moyal-Sharrock, 24–47, Leiden: Brill.
  (2017). 'Fighting Relativism: Wittgenstein and Kuhn', in *Realism – Relativism – Constructivism* (eds.) C. Kanzian, S. Kletzl & K. Neges, 215–32, Berlin: de Gruyter.

(2019). 'Wittgenstein's Grammar: Through Thick and Thin', in *Wittgensteinian (adj.): Looking at the World from the Viewpoint of Wittgenstein's Philosophy* (eds.) S. Wuppuluri & N. da Costa, 39–54, Dordrecht: Springer.

(2021*a*). 'Restoring Certainty', *International Journal for the Study of Skepticism* 11, 143–58.

(2021*b*). *Certainty in Action: Wittgenstein on Language, Mind & Epistemology*, London: Bloomsbury.

Nielsen, K. (1967). 'Wittgensteinian Fideism', *Philosophy* 42, 237–54.

Nozick, R. (1981). *Philosophical Explanations*, Oxford: Oxford University Press.

O'Hara, N. (2018). *Moral Certainty and the Foundations of Morality*, London: Palgrave Macmillan.

Phillips, D. Z. (1976). *Religion without Explanation*, Oxford: Oxford University Press.

Pleasants, N. (2008). 'Wittgenstein, Ethics and Basic Moral Certainty', *Inquiry* 51, 241–67.

Pritchard, D. H. (2002). 'Two Forms of Epistemological Contextualism', *Grazer Philosophische Studien* 64, 19–55.

(2005). *Epistemic Luck*, Oxford: Oxford University Press.

(2010*a*). 'Epistemic Relativism, Epistemic Incommensurability and Wittgensteinian Epistemology', in *The Blackwell Companion to Relativism* (ed.) S. Hales, 266–85, Oxford: Blackwell.

(2010*b*). 'Relevant Alternatives, Perceptual Knowledge, and Discrimination', *Noûs* 44, 245–68.

(2011*a*). 'Wittgenstein on Scepticism', in *Oxford Handbook on Wittgenstein* (eds.) O. Kuusela & M. McGinn, 521–47, Oxford: Oxford University Press.

(2011*b*). 'Wittgensteinian Quasi-Fideism', *Oxford Studies in the Philosophy of Religion* 4, 145–59.

(2012*a*). *Epistemological Disjunctivism*, Oxford: Oxford University Press.

(2012*b*). 'Wittgenstein and the Groundlessness of Our Believing', *Synthese* 189, 255–72.

(2015*a*). *Epistemic Angst: Radical Skepticism and the Groundlessness of Our Believing*, Princeton, NJ: Princeton University Press.

(2015*b*). 'Wittgenstein on Faith and Reason: The Influence of Newman', in *God, Truth and Other Enigmas* (ed.) M. Szatkowski, 141–64, Berlin: DeGruyter.

(2017*a*). 'Faith and Reason', *Philosophy* 81, 101–18.

(2017*b*). 'Wittgenstein on Hinge Commitments and Radical Scepticism in *On Certainty*', in *Blackwell Companion to Wittgenstein* (eds.) H.-J. Glock & J. Hyman, 563–75, Oxford: Blackwell.

(2018*a*). 'Disagreement, of Belief and Otherwise', in *Voicing Dissent: The Ethics and Epistemology of Making Disagreement Public* (ed.) C. Johnson, 22–39, London: Routledge.

(2018*b*). 'Epistemic *Angst*', *Philosophy and Phenomenological Research* 96, 70–90.

(2018*c*). 'Quasi-Fideism and Religious Conviction', *European Journal for Philosophy of Religion* 10, 51–66.

(2018*d*). 'Unnatural Doubts', in *Skepticism: Historical and Contemporary Inquiries* (eds.) G. A. Bruno & A. Rutherford, 223–47, London: Routledge.

(2018*e*). 'Wittgensteinian Hinge Epistemology and Deep Disagreement', *Topoi* 40, 1117–25. https://doi.org/10.1007/s11245-018-9612-y.

(2019*a*). 'Wittgensteinian Epistemology, Epistemic Vertigo, and Pyrrhonian Scepticism', in *Epistemology after Sextus Empiricus* (eds.) J. Vlasits & K. M. Vogt, 172–92, Oxford: Oxford University Press.

(2019*b*). 'Wittgenstein's *on Certainty* as Pyrrhonism in Action', in *Wittgensteinian (adj.): Looking at Things from the Viewpoint of Wittgenstein's Philosophy* (eds.) N. de Costa & S. Wuppuluri, 91–106, Dordrecht: Springer.

(2020). 'Epistemic Vertigo', in *The Philosophy and Psychology of Ambivalence: Being of Two Minds*, (eds.) B. Brogaard & D. Gatzia, 110–128, London: Routledge.

(2021*a*). 'Cavell and Philosophical Vertigo', *Journal for the History of Analytic Philosophy* 9, 7–22.

(2021*b*). 'Ignorance and Inquiry', *American Philosophical Quarterly* 58, 111–23.

(2021*c*). 'Ignorance and Normativity', *Philosophical Topics* 49, 225–43.

(2021*d*). 'Sceptical Fideism and Quasi-Fideism', *Manuscrito* 44, 3–30.

(2022*a*). 'Exploring Quasi-Fideism', in *Extending Hinge Epistemology*, (eds.) D. Moyal-Sharrock & C. Sandis, 26–48, London: Anthem.

(2022*b*). 'Hinge Commitments and Common Knowledge', *Synthese*. https://doi.org/10.1007/s11229-022-03647-5.

(2022*c*). 'In Defence of Closure', in *New Perspectives on Epistemic Closure*, (eds.) M. Jope & D. H. Pritchard, 113–30, London: Routledge.

(2022*d*). 'Quasi-Fideism and Epistemic Relativism', *Inquiry*. https://doi.org/10.1080/0020174X.2022.2135820.

(2023*a*). 'Hinge Commitments and Trust', *Synthese*. https://doi.org/10.1007/s11229-023-04378-x.

(2023*b*). 'Understanding Deep Disagreement', *International Journal of Philosophical Studies*. https://doi.org/10.1080/09672559.2023.2263709.

(2024a). 'Religious Vertigo', in *Religionsphilosophie nach Wittgenstein (Philosophy of Religion after Wittgenstein)*, (ed.) E. Ramharter, 287–306. Stuttgart: Metzler/Springer.

(2024b). 'Epistemic Vertigo and Existential *Angst*', *Conversations: Journal of Cavellian Studies* 11, 17–36.

(2024c). 'Beliefs, Delusions, Hinge Commitments', *Synthese* 204, https://doi.org/10.1007/s11229-024-04703-y.

(2024d). 'Hume and Wittgenstein on Naturalism and Scepticism', in *Hume and Contemporary Epistemology*, (eds.) S. Stapleford & V. Wagner, 206–20, London: Routledge.

(2025). 'Deep Disagreement', in *Routledge Handbook to Philosophy of Disagreement*, (eds.) M. Baghramian, J. A. Carter & R. Rowland, ch. 4, 31–61, London: Routledge.

(*Forthcominga*). 'Honest Doubt: Quasi-Fideism and Epistemic Vertigo', in *Wittgenstein and the Epistemology of Religion*, (eds.) D. H. Pritchard & N. Venturinha, Oxford: Oxford University Press.

(*Forthcomingb*). 'Pyrrhonism and Wittgensteinian Quietism', in *Ancient Scepticism and Contemporary Philosophy*, (eds.) L. Perissinotto & B. R. Cámara, Milan: Mimesis International.

(*Forthcomingc*). 'Quasi-Fideism and Virtuous Anti-Evidentialism: Wittgenstein and Newman on Knowledge and Certainty', in *Newman and Contemporary Philosophy*, (eds.) J. Milburn & F. Aquino, London: Routledge.

(*Forthcomingd*). 'Strawson and Wittgenstein on Hinge Commitments', in *Skepticism and Naturalism: Hume, Wittgenstein, Strawson*, (eds.) J. Hyman, Y. Ohta & M. Thorne, Leiden: Brill.

Putnam, H. (1998). 'Strawson and Skepticism', in *The Philosophy of P. F. Strawson*, (ed.) L. E. Hahn, 273–87, Chicago, IL: Open Court.

Ranalli, C. (2020). 'Deep Disagreement and Hinge Epistemology', *Synthese* 197, 4975–5007.

(2021a). 'Are There Heavyweight Perceptual Reasons?', *International Journal for the Study of Skepticism* 11, 93–118.

(2021b). 'Moral Hinges and Steadfastness', *Metaphilosophy* 52, 379–401.

Read, R., & Lavery, M. (eds.). (2011). *Beyond the Tractatus Wars: The New Wittgenstein Debate*, London: Routledge.

Russell, B. (1910). 'Knowledge by Acquaintance and Knowledge by Description', *Proceedings of the Aristotelian Society* 11, 108–128.

Russell, B. (1912). *Problems of Philosophy*, (ed.) J. Perry, Oxford: Oxford University Press.

Sandis, C., & Moyal-Sharrock, D. (eds.). (2022). *Extending Hinge Epistemology*, London: Anthem.

Schönbaumsfeld, G. (2016). *The Illusion of Doubt*, Oxford: Oxford University Press.
  (2017). 'Beliefs-in-a-Vat', *Proceedings of the Aristotelian Society* 117, 141–61.
  (2019). 'Was Wittgenstein a Disjunctivist *Avant la Lettre*?', in *New Issues in Epistemological Disjunctivism*, (eds.) C. Doyle, J. Milburn & D. H. Pritchard, 113–30, London: Routledge.
  (2021*a*). '*Précis* of *The Illusion of Doubt*', *International Journal for the Study of Skepticism* 11, 87–92.
  (2021*b*). 'Response to Critics (Ranalli, Williams, Moyal-Sharrock)', *International Journal for the Study of Skepticism* 11, 159–75.
Schroeder, S. (2024) 'Farewell to Hinge Propositions' in his *Language, Mind, and Value: Essays on Wittgenstein*, 145–60, London: Anthem.
Siegel, H. (2021). 'Hinges, Disagreements, and Arguments: (Rationally) Believing Hinge Propositions and Arguing across Deep Disagreements', *Topoi* 40, 1107–16.
Sluga, H. (2004). 'Wittgenstein and Pyrrhonism', in *Pyrrhonian Skepticism*, (ed.) W. Sinnott-Armstrong, 99–117, Oxford: Oxford University Press.
Smith, N. (2021). 'How to Hang a Door: Picking Hinges for Quasi-Fideism', *European Journal for Philosophy of Religion* 13, 51–82.
Sosa, E. (1998). 'P. F. Strawson's Epistemological Naturalism', in *The Philosophy of P. F. Strawson*, (ed.) L. E. Hahn, 361–69, Chicago, IL: Open Court.
Stern, R. (2003). 'On Strawson's Naturalistic Turn', in *Strawson and Kant*, (ed.) H.-J. Glock, 219–34, Oxford: Oxford University Press.
Stevenson, L. (2002). 'Six Levels of Mentality', *Philosophical Explorations* 5, 105–24.
Strawson, P. F. (1959). *Individuals*, London: Methuen.
  (1966). *The Bounds of Sense: An Essay on Kant's Critique of Pure Reason*, London: Methuen.
  (1985). *Skepticism and Naturalism: Some Varieties*, New York: Columbia University Press.
  (1998*a*). 'Reply to Ernest Sosa', in *The Philosophy of P. F. Strawson*, (ed.) L. E. Hahn, 370–72, Chicago, IL: Open Court.
  (1998*b*). 'Reply to Hilary Putnam', in *The Philosophy of P. F. Strawson*, (ed.) L. E. Hahn, 288–92, Chicago IL: Open Court.
Stroll, A. (1994). *Moore and Wittgenstein on Certainty*, Oxford: Oxford University Press.
Stroll, A. (2002). 'Understanding on Certainty: Entry 194', in *Wittgenstein and the Future of Philosophy*, (eds.) R. Haller, & K. Puhl, 446–56, Vienna: oebvhpt.

Stroud. B. (1984). *The Significance of Philosophical Scepticism*, Oxford: Clarendon Press.

Svensson, G. (1981). *On Doubting the Reality of Reality: Moore and Wittgenstein on Sceptical Doubts*, Stockholm: Almqvist & Wiksell.

Thébert, A. (2023). 'Peut-on comprendre le sceptique?', *Revue de metaphysique et de morale* 3, 311–33.

Tiercelin, C. (2010). 'Peirce et Wittgenstein: deux strategies pragmatistes face au defi sceptique', *Paradigmi* 3, 13–28.

van Gennip, K. (2008) 'Wittgenstein's on Certainty in the Making: Studies into Its Historical and Philosophical Background' PhD thesis, University of Groningen.

von Wright, G. H. (1982). *Wittgenstein*, Minneapolis: University of Minnesota Press.

Varela, F. J., Thompson, E. & Rosch, E. (1991). *The Embodied Mind: Cognitive Science and Human Experience*. Cambridge, MA: The MIT Press.

Vinten, R. (2022). 'Wittgenstein, Quasi-Fideism, and Scepticism', *Topoi* 41, 967–78 https://doi.org/10.1007/s11245-022-09832-y.

Williams, M. (1991). *Unnatural Doubts: Epistemological Realism and the Basis of Scepticism*, Oxford: Blackwell.

(2004). 'Wittgenstein's Refutation of Idealism', in *Wittgenstein and Scepticism*, (ed.) D. McManus, 76–96, London: Routledge.

(2017). 'How Hinges Can Be Knowledge', *manuscript*.

(2018). 'Illusions of Doubt: Wittgenstein on Knowledge and Certainty', in *Skepticism: from Antiquity to the Present*, (eds.) D. Machuca & B. Reed, 371–89, London: Bloomsbury.

(2021*a*). 'No Shadow of a Doubt: Wittgenstein on Knowledge and Certainty; Neglected Themes', *Midwest Studies in Philosophy* 45, 179–208.

(2021*b*). 'Knowledge without "Experience"', *International Journal for the Study of Skepticism* 11, 119–42.

(*Forthcoming*). 'Fideism, Skepticism and "Hinge" Epistemology', in *Wittgenstein and the Epistemology of Religion*, (eds.) D. H. Pritchard & N. Venturinha, Oxford: Oxford University Press.

Williamson, T. (2000). *Knowledge and Its Limits*, Oxford: Oxford University Press.

Wright, C. (2004*a*). 'Hinge Propositions and the Serenity Prayer', in *Knowledge and Belief, Proceedings of the 26th International Wittgenstein Symposium*, (eds.) W. Loffler & P. Weingartner, 287–306, Vienna: Holder-Pickler-Tempsky.

(2004*b*). 'Warrant for Nothing (and Foundations for Free)?', *Proceedings of the Aristotelian Society* (supp.) 78, 167–212.

(2022). 'Closure and Transmission Again', in *New Perspectives on Epistemic Closure*, (eds.) M. Jope & D. H. Pritchard, 163–90, London: Routledge.

Wittgenstein, L. (1966). *Wittgenstein's Lectures and Conversations on Aesthetics, Psychology and Religious Belief*, (ed.) C. Barrett, Oxford: Basil Blackwell.

Cambridge Elements =

The Philosophy of Ludwig Wittgenstein

David G. Stern
University of Iowa

David G. Stern is a Professor of Philosophy and a Collegiate Fellow in the College of Liberal Arts and Sciences at the University of Iowa. His research interests include history of analytic philosophy, philosophy of language, philosophy of mind, and philosophy of science. He is the author of *Wittgenstein's Philosophical Investigations: An Introduction* (Cambridge University Press, 2004) and *Wittgenstein on Mind and Language* (Oxford University Press, 1995), as well as more than 50 journal articles and book chapters. He is the editor of *Wittgenstein in the 1930s: Between the 'Tractatus' and the 'Investigations'* (Cambridge University Press, 2018) and is also a co-editor of the *Cambridge Companion to Wittgenstein* (Cambridge University Press, 2nd edition, 2018), *Wittgenstein: Lectures, Cambridge 1930–1933, from the Notes of G. E. Moore* (Cambridge University Press, 2016) and *Wittgenstein Reads Weininger* (Cambridge University Press, 2004).

About the Series
This series provides concise and structured introductions to all the central topics in the philosophy of Ludwig Wittgenstein. The Elements are written by distinguished senior scholars and bright junior scholars with relevant expertise, producing balanced and comprehensive coverage of the full range of Wittgenstein's thought.

Cambridge Elements

The Philosophy of Ludwig Wittgenstein

Elements in the Series

Wittgenstein on Logic and Philosophical Method
Oskari Kuusela

Wittgenstein on Sense and Grammar
Silver Bronzo

Wittgenstein on Forms of Life
Anna Boncompagni

Wittgenstein on Criteria and Practices
Lars Hertzberg

Wittgenstein on Religious Belief
Genia Schönbaumsfeld

Wittgenstein and Aesthetics
Hanne Appelqvist

Style, Method and Philosophy in Wittgenstein
Alois Pichler

Wittgenstein on Realism and Idealism
David R. Cerbone

Wittgenstein and Ethics
Anne-Marie Søndergaard Christensen

Wittgenstein and Russell
Sanford Shieh

Wittgenstein on Music
Eran Guter

Wittgenstein on Knowledge and Certainty
Danièle Moyal-Sharrock and Duncan Pritchard

A full series listing is available at: www.cambridge.org/EPLW

Printed in Dunstable, United Kingdom